Also by the author

The Place of Precious Things

This Mystery and I

The Quiet Place Within

The Little Book of Awareness

Transforming Negative Emotions

The Heart of Awareness

pantheonprosebooks.com

TALKS WITH TEMERLEN

An exploration into the deeper meaning
of consciousness, meditation, and prayer

PETER INGLE

Copyright © 2017–2023 Peter Ingle

TALKS WITH TEMERLEN

All rights reserved

ISBN 978-0-9746349-6-8
ISBN-13: 978-0974634968 (Peter Ingle)

No part of this publication may be reproduced,
stored, or transmitted in any form or by any means
electronic, mechanical, photocopying, recording,
or otherwise, without written permission from
the author.

Published in the United States of America
Library of Congress Cataloging-in-Publication Data

Ingle, Peter M.
TALKS WITH TEMERLEN

Awareness is Everything 1
Who is Temerlen Gillis? 11
Prayer as Meditation 13
Prayer as an Appeal 15
Prayer as Bold Magic 19
Silent Congregation 22
Insights as Patchwork 25
Truth 28
The Tone of The Lord's Prayer 29
The Mind Can Only Think God 32
A Circle of Unity 35
Prayer as a Path 37
Hidden Truth 40
Why Church? 44
Do Water and Sunlight Pray? 49
Gender and Unity in The Lord's Prayer 51
Life and Awareness 54
Different Religions 56
The Bible and Technology 58
Where is The Kingdom? 62
Line by Line 67

Another Perspective 73
The Prayer in Reverse 77
Bread, Debts, and Sins 80
The Identity of Awareness 88
Heaven and Earth 91
Temptation and Evil 94
Awareness is Elusive to Itself 98
Slipping Out of the Mind 102
Prodigal Awareness 107
Sharing Insights 116
Awareness is Invisible 121
The Passenger 126
Prayer, Meditation, and Yoga 134
The Bible, Religion, and Light 136
World Without End 143

The words have remained,
but their meaning has been long lost.

George Ivanovich Gurdjieff

Talks With Temerlen

Awareness is Everything

IT WAS TIME to start the interview. Sitting in my chair in the recording studio, I felt unusually nervous. My guest would be a professor named Temerlen P. Gillis who had lectured at the local college a week before on the subject of awareness. There was something unusual about his manner that had drawn me in, so after his talk I asked if he might join my weekly show sometime for an interview, to which he agreed.

The focal point of our interview was going to be the nature of awareness which he had touched on during his lecture and which I had found intriguing due to his simple way of explaining a subject that many people presume to understand, but which he cast in a whole new light.

As I sat reviewing my questions, the door opened and in walked a slender, graying man in his late 60s with a gentle face and calm manner. Mr. Gillis looked at me knowingly, walked to my chair, and shook my hand. He then took a seat, got comfortable in front of the microphone, lifted the glass of water in front of him, and took a sip. I asked if he was ready to begin and he nodded with a smile.

I read my introduction about him as a professor of philosophy who had for many years studied religion and eastern spirituality. I then looked at him and asked if he could describe for our listeners the nature of human awareness and why he felt it was so important.

With his hands folded quietly in front of him and with no sign of hesitation, he began by explaining that simple awareness—the capacity in humans to be aware—is the most remarkable yet most overlooked fact about our existence. "Awareness is everything," he said, "but because it's *behind* everything else about our existence we don't notice it."

"And yet," I responded, "you and I are aware that we're here doing this interview, and everyone listening is aware that they're hearing it. Isn't this what you mean?"

"Yes and no," Mr. Gillis said. "It's true that, as we're talking, we're aware and your listeners are aware. In this sense, we're all naturally aware. At the same time—and this is the key—awareness is not aware of being aware; it's not consciously aware."

The he added: "And just my saying this caused your awareness to jump up a notch."

"As a matter of fact," I replied. "I did feel something."

"Can you describe it," he asked. "What did you feel?"

After a pause, I said, "Well, for one thing, it became more obvious—if that's the word—that we're sitting here."

"Anything else?" he asked.

"Yes," I said. "You became more vivid. I saw you and heard you more vividly."

"True," replied Mr. Gillis. "Everything you just said happens when awareness becomes more aware. But there's something else. Did you catch it?"

At his question, I felt myself go on guard, as though I had to solve a riddle. "Well," I said, "I suppose I became more vivid, too; more aware of being in the studio with you. Is that what you mean?"

"Almost," he said. "Very close. In fact, what's so interesting about your description is that it's very close, but only close. Most people who are asked the same thing also come very close.

"Think of it like this," he continued. "A moment ago, *what* you were aware of became more vivid. You suddenly became more aware of me and more aware of you. At the same time—and this is what gets missed—awareness became aware of *itself*. This coming home of awareness, this being aware of being aware, is the hallmark of spiritual life. Everything else is just talk.

"You have to realize," Mr. Gillis said slowly, "how odd it is that awareness is always here and always aware, yet seldom is it aware of being aware. I say odd because the more you notice this, the more you realize that everything else about our existence stems from awareness, depends on awareness, and pales in significance to awareness. But we don't give this any attention or talk about it. We take awareness completely for granted."

He then paused. His gaze lowered as he seemed to journey deep into thought. He seemed unhurried, as though waiting for thoughts to reveal themselves rather than chasing after something scripted to say. He clearly wasn't concerned about the delay in our broadcast, as I was.

Just as I was about to speak, he continued:

"Of course, what we're talking about—the nature of awareness—is beyond the mind's ability to grasp it. The mind is more limited than we like to believe. That's why it's good to talk about awareness. Talking about awareness pushes the mind up against its own limits, and sometimes beyond.

"You see," he continued, "the mind can only *think* about awareness. It can only conceptualize it. The mind cannot be aware. Take right now, for example. As our minds use words to construct a mental notion of something called awareness, we're aware this is going on. There's thinking and there's awareness of thinking—two phenomena. One mentally tangible. The other intangible and elusive to the mind."

"It seems obvious when you point it out," I said. "But most of the time I don't notice this distinction. Frankly, I've never even thought about it."

"Precisely," he replied, "and it's interesting how you just said it: that you don't 'notice' it. In other words, awareness goes unnoticed most of the time. Isn't that strange? And to whom does it go unnoticed? To itself.

"Look carefully," he went on, "and you'll see that you can be aware of your hands, you can be aware that you're talking or walking, you can be aware that you see, hear, taste, touch, and smell. But none of these activities or senses can be aware of themselves. Only awareness can be aware of them. For example, your hand is not aware of itself. Your eyes are not aware of seeing. Something else is aware of them. And only that can be aware of *itself*."

After a pause, Mr. Gillis continued: "This capacity to be aware of being aware seems so simple, doesn't it—so ridiculously simple—yet this is the essence of enlightenment.

"Imagine," he continued, "what such awareness would be like on the scale of our galaxy or universe, or beyond—an infinite awareness encompassing everything else."

"You mean God," I said.

"I mean awareness," Mr. Gillis said softly. "Larger and larger and larger awareness that is more and more and more conscious of being aware of being aware."

"But what else can that be but God?" I said.

"Ultimately," he replied, "you acknowledge that what we call God is awareness and that awareness is God."

"Wouldn't awareness be the presence of God?" I asked. "In the sense that God is beyond awareness, bigger than awareness?"

"It's an interesting question," said Mr. Gillis. "And it's interesting that it's not asked more often or examined more carefully."

"You mean we take God for granted," I said.

"I would say," he replied, "that we make too many assumptions about what God is, just as we make too many assumptions about who and what we are."

After a pause, he went on: "You have to realize that the concept of God has different meaning for different people. This in itself is interesting.

Why are they so different? How can there be differences where something as big as God is concerned?

"At the same time," he added, "God is usually considered to be physically out of reach. Just from this point of view it's worth asking: where is God, what form does God actually take, and what precisely is his relationship to us? These sound like reasonable questions, but they challenge assumptions that we take for granted. But why should we settle for assumptions on such an important issue?"

I then asked, "What about God as awareness? Can't we ask the same questions?"

"We can," said Mr. Gillis, "and we should. But we have to understand that it's the mind which poses such questions. The mind asks about God from the mind's frame of reference, which is all it knows, then it shapes answers within that frame. The mind is remarkable, but when you step out of it, you see that the mind is a box you can put a lot of stuff into, but it can't get outside of itself. The mind is very much its own trap.

"Nevertheless," Mr. Gillis said, "the mind can

visualize things beyond itself—like the solar system, the galaxy, and the universe. It can then conclude that everything is connected; that the universe is an enormous body; that even though all the parts seem disconnected, they're really one because together they form one large whole."

I then asked: "So what and where is God in all this?"

He didn't respond right away. He just looked at me thoughtfully. After a few moments, he said, "You might say that God is ultimate awareness and that each human being contains a potential of awareness, and that in their purest form they are the same."

"And what about prayer?" I said.

"Prayer," he responded right away, "is a link between the two: between potential awareness and full, conscious awareness. What's important to understand, though, is that prayer doesn't belong to awareness. Awareness is already aware. It has no need of prayer, which is a mental exercise. Prayer exists as a vehicle for the mind to open itself—yield itself—to awareness. In religious terms, this is man surrendering to the will of God. In reality, it means the mind surrendering to awareness so that awareness will recognize itself, realize itself, return to itself.

"In its highest form," Mr. Gillis continued, "prayer is an appeal by the mind to awareness in the sincere hope that awareness will actualize itself as conscious awareness by becoming aware of being aware."

"So, we're really praying to ourselves, not to God." I said.

"Yes and no," he said. "We as physical beings are petitioning metaphysical awareness to be consciously aware. You might say that we're pleading to God to save us by saving himself. This is the only true salvation. There is no external salvation. And when you take the concept of God out of the equation, it's strictly about awareness. Behind the universe, encompassing the universe, and filling the universe is pure awareness. You can still call it God and pray to it, but as soon as pure awareness recognizes itself, all that falls away."

Who is Temerlen Gillis?

Well, you can imagine the feedback the station got from this broadcast:

Who is this Temerlen Gillis?

Since when does this guy have the authority to dismiss religion wholesale and claim we are God?

Awareness, smareness. This is your usual spirituality speak and new-age gobbledy gook.

For other listeners, it was a revelation:

Completely blown away. I was forced to take a hard look at all this. Wow.

Needless to say, praying didn't feel the same after listening to Mr. Gillis. It felt better and meant more.

I applaud his daring honesty. He just shot what feels like an arrow of truth into the heart of my belief system. I hope that's a good thing.

I stayed in touch with Mr. Gillis, at first by phone. He didn't want to do another live broadcast, but he said he would be interested in some private recording sessions. Of course, I agreed. He felt to me like a fresh spring of knowledge and I wanted to bottle some of it.

As it turned out, what Mr. Gillis really wanted was to explore the idea of prayer, specifically The Lord's Prayer. He said he wanted to peel away the literal meaning and examine its metaphysical purpose.

What follows is a record of our talks on this subject over a period of several months.

Something to keep in mind while reading these "snapshots" is that Mr. Gillis was never in a hurry. He never insisted on his point of view. He never tried to convince me of anything. On the contrary, he always spoke carefully, often pausing as he went, never pressing to reach a conclusion. His demeanor left the impression of someone paddling a canoe down a tranquil stream with ease and precision. His thoughts were like deep, slow strokes that propelled us along. Occasionally he would make two or three incisive strokes and let us glide downstream. Never did he seem lost and never did he say where we were going, which always came as a wonderful, sometimes startling, surprise.

Prayer as Meditation

Our first session began with Temerlen saying that The Lord's Prayer is a form of meditation.

"This terse prayer," he said, "appears almost without notice in the Gospels, yet it has come to represent the capstone and core of Christianity. It compresses an entire religion into roughly 50 words and about 30 seconds of invocation that are presumed to be a direct appeal to the supreme being. Think for a moment what this means.

"You are a human being on a planet in a solar system inside a galaxy that sails through a vast universe. You call to thought a 'prayer' and recite it as though speaking to the most absolute being of that universe. This is an invocation and meditation of the highest order. Wouldn't you think that each syllable of each word demands the utmost scrutiny and respect?"

"Where did The Lord's Prayer come from?" I asked.

"I'm not sure," Temerlen said. "And I'm not sure anyone knows. It's thought that the Gospels weren't written until 50 or 100 or more years after the supposed life of Jesus. That's a long time, so this prayer may not even have come from someone named Jesus, but from the authors, whoever they were. The real question is, what gives this prayer so much power?

"And these raise other questions," he continued. "For example, who is the 'Lord'? Who is 'us'? Where is the 'kingdom'? What are daily bread and debts? What is temptation and is it unavoidable? Above all, are we to understand these things literally, or does the outer meaning conceal a hidden purpose? If so, where exactly is The Lord's Prayer supposed to lead 'us'?"

Temerlen looked at me, not expecting an answer to his surge of provocative questions, but rather watching to see how I was going to navigate the unexpected door he had just opened in front of me. His silent gaze seemed to suggest that, for now at least, it was enough just to be posing all these questions.

Prayer as an Appeal

After a short break, Temerlen started peeling away more assumptions.

"At first glance," he said, "The Lord's Prayer is an appeal to God. I am 'here', God is out 'there', and I ask for his help, for his forgiveness, or for something that I believe only God can grant. The prayer can even be viewed as the beginning of a conversation with God. I start talking. God listens. Maybe God answers. Maybe not.

"The prayer is also a form of surrender. It says, God, you are large and powerful and compassionate. I am small and helpless and in need of your grace. I surrender to you and let you take charge. Through this exchange, I feel relief, freedom, even joy and love.

"Appealing to, conversing with, and surrendering to God evokes religious emotion. We feel better. We feel lighter. We feel supported. We may even feel a sense of goodness about mankind, at least for a time.

"Given all this, it's worth asking what really happens when we invoke this prayer—or any prayer. What's the effect on us, how does it happen, why does it require prayer to make it happen? And beyond the usual beliefs about prayer, is there anything more? Something deeper? Something more profound?

"What if," he continued, "The Lord's Prayer is more than a dialogue and an appeal? What if it's a blueprint—a psychological map—for an inner journey? What if we start to realize that this prayer is not meant to bring us closer to God 'out there' but instead to guide us through the caverns of our psyche and propel awareness beyond the sense of identity we usually dwell in?

"In other words," said Temerlen, "what if this prayer is a tool given to the mind for the purpose of evoking awareness—pure awareness conscious of itself apart from thought?"

I then asked, "But where does that leave God?"

"It changes the definition of God," said Temerlen, "doesn't it?"

"It changes everything," I replied.

"It does," he said. Then he paused for a long

while before resuming.

"The generally accepted meaning of The Lord's Prayer," he said, "is that Jesus is the Lord who taught the prayer to his disciples as a way of appealing to God, his Father. The implication is that God watches over those who admit their temptations and sins—which God will forgive if you ask him to.

"In the larger context, God is in 'heaven' and passage from earth to heaven is facilitated through prayer, which concludes in 'salvation' at death. The Lord's Prayer is a way to communicate with God who responds according to a person's degree of devotion. The more devoted you are, the more God listens. If you ask forgiveness, you'll be 'saved'. If you don't, you go to Hell as a non-believer who succumbed to God's nemesis, the Devil.

"As soon as we say all this out loud," he continued, "it sounds absurd, doesn't it? Yet these beliefs are readily adopted by the mind and never questioned with rigor."

I replied: "The more you describe it, the more peculiar it seems."

"Yes," said Temerlen, "and all we did was poke at the literal meaning."

"And you want to keep poking don't you," I said.

He was silent.

After gazing down for a moment, he looked back at me. "What I want," he said, "is to shine light on the truth. There is a deeper truth behind this prayer and within this prayer."

Prayer as Bold Magic

One morning after we'd done a short recording, Temerlen went for a walk by himself. When he returned, he sat down, adjusted his microphone, and nodded for me to start the recording again.

"There's nothing arbitrary about The Lord's Prayer," he said. "It wasn't conceived on impulse. It was put together with great care for a specific reason. The wording contains deep understanding and the more you delve into it, the more you see how much is packed into this small bundle of words. It's more than a comforting recitation. It's an incantation of metaphysical magic."

The words 'incantation' and 'magic' caught me by surprise. They added a strange flavor to the idea of prayer. Temerlen saw my frown and seemed to know what I was thinking.

"They're strange words," he said, "because we're not accustomed to thinking about prayer as a potion. We've been taught to believe that prayer is directed outward to God. But when you turn prayer inward, this changes. God, if he still exists, is then inside you. What is that? Where is that? These are the things we want to know.

These are what The Lord's Prayer is designed to show us."

He continued: "The Lord's Prayer can make you feel better, but it's capable of much more. It can transform you. More accurately, it can transform awareness. The question is how well you understand this and how to what degree you can commandeer the prayer to achieve it.

"In the Gospels, Jesus taught his disciples how to pray. He even added the advice, 'Ask and it shall be given to you' and 'Enter into your closet when you pray'. Something particular is at stake. Something more than forgiveness. What exactly will be 'given'. And where is this closet? How do you 'enter' into it?

"When this is understood," he went on, "The Lord's Prayer becomes the most dynamic tool the Gospels have to offer. It becomes more than supplication because it's more than a conversation with God. In its highest form, it's an exchange between the mind and the higher self of awareness. It's the mind trying to invoke and evoke conscious awareness."

After a pause, he added: "Or maybe it's a way for awareness to use the mind as a lever to lift itself up to and into conscious awareness. In any case, harnessing The Lord's Prayer signifies a particular inner action the same way that the Golden Rule is a particular outer action. Neither one is for its own sake, but for the sake of something beyond itself. They're both about awareness—in ourselves and in others."

Then he said, "The hardest thing is getting rid of the image of God as a person out 'there' who can do something for you. Human nature has a long root that extends deep inside where it's tied to a core of fear and insecurity. We want someone or something to take care of us, to protect us, to save us. This is the core of the psyche and awareness is tied to it, unaware that it can slip free at any time. The reason slipping free is difficult is because awareness isn't aware of itself. Becoming aware of being aware unties the knot. And that's what prayer is for."

I replied, "This creates a very different image of people praying."

"Yes," said Temerlen. "People are no longer searching for God to save them. They're looking within for the key to set themselves free."

Silent Congregation

After a short break, Temerlen returned to the idea that awareness may use The Lord's Prayer as a kind of lever.

"Just envision," he said, "a Sunday morning congregation. Instead of everyone simply repeating The Lord's Prayer, imagine the church in complete silence: each person internalizing the prayer, everyone taking it at their own pace, chewing on each word, searching to uncover its deeper meaning.

"There would be no need for a sermon," he continued, "other than to remind everyone to do exactly what we're talking about—to find their way into their 'closet' and induce a self-transformation—a metamorphosis—of awareness. Each person would quietly leave the church when they felt ready to step back into the 'world'."

I quipped: "Church might not be so popular then."

"Probably not," said Temerlen. "People have a hard time staying silent for very long, especially when they're with other people. Our fear of silence and the discomfort of silence is also what keeps the door to our 'closet' closed. Sometimes you have to walk down a corridor of discomfort and fear to reach that door. Then you have to know how to open the door and walk in. And you have to know why you're doing it. You have to have a reason for using The Lord's Prayer."

"Prayer," I said, "is also unique to humans. I mean, it's obvious when you think about it, but plants and animals can't pray."

"All forms of life in the universe," replied Temerlen. "embody the substance of their source, their 'Father'. But not all of them, as far as we know, have the ability to acknowledge their source. So the human mind is some kind of rare faculty—a piece of specialized equipment in the universe—that awareness can pass through and become aware of itself as being the same substance as its source."

After a brief pause, he added, "You see how this changes the notion of God? It dispenses with a physical god in the universe. It also gives fresh meaning to the idea of man 'formed in god's image', and to concepts like 'salvation' and 'resurrection' and 'heaven'. When we turn the idea of prayer inward, prayer becomes a conduit, a loop, through which awareness circulates for its own health. It represents awareness using the mind to have a conscious exchange with itself, which may be the best description of what meditation is in its purest form. And it's undoubtedly what eastern mystics meant about Brahman continuously breathing himself in and out. They weren't referring to just the physical universe. They meant awareness *consciously* issuing itself and *consciously* returning to itself."

He then added: "The mind can't grasp this 'substance' of awareness, but this substance can pass through the mind, and whoever invented prayer knew this. They also knew that bowing the head really refers to the mind deferring to awareness; that kneeling means the body yielding to awareness; that clasping or folding the hands means concentrating all energy internally and not allowing it to disperse through extraneous movement, sensation, thought, or emotion—to contain and 'hold' one's finest energy inside for the sake of transformation.

We both sat in silence as the recording continued, but Temerlen said nothing more.

Insights as Patchwork

(from my notes after a walk with Temerlen)

One afternoon after we had been recording, Temerlen suggested a short walk. It was, as usual with him, a relaxed walk, not 'walking' for exercise. As we went, we kept silent. After a bit, I asked, "Why have you never tried to write down all your perceptions about The Lord's Prayer? Maybe publish it as a series of articles or a book on the subject?"

Temerlen kept walking and said, "I thought of that until we did our radio interview. I had been struggling with writing but nothing was coming together. After our interview I realized it was because this material—these perceptions as you call them—don't belong to the mind. We can describe awareness conceptually, but the concepts always remain at a distance from awareness itself. The mind itself can never grasp the thing it conceptualizes.

"That's why," he continued, "I could never organize my perceptions into a logical stream. They're not logical. Or rather, they're beyond logic. And because of that, they resist mental organization. It's like trying to scoop water with your hands. You manage to get some, but not all of it. And if you toss it in the air, it's gone, dispersed right away. It doesn't stay together."

Then he added, "During our first interview, I was surprised how well things came together. We managed to capture something vital, don't you think? That's when I realized that all these perceptions are fragments of insight from awareness. They travel through the mind, but the mind can't hang onto them as a single stream. But, when we pass these perceptions back and forth between our two minds we manage to keep a thread going and things become more visible, almost tangible."

We continued walking in silence.

"It's a good thing," he then said, "that these perceptions can't be fully contained by the mind. Otherwise the mind would claim them as its own. By eluding the mind, they require awareness to become conscious of itself watching the mind—to become aware of being aware above the mind."

Temerlen slowed down, stopped, and turned toward me.

"It's important to understand that awareness is not a person or identity. It has no claim on anything, no immersion in anything. It's not in pursuit of anything. It is simply pure, unalloyed awareness with the ability to be conscious of itself. The mind doesn't possess this ability."

He stood quietly for a moment, looking at the ground.

"You see," he then said, "it's already too many words. It's good to talk about awareness, but too many words and awareness starts to slip away. This is why it's right to enter your 'closet' and retreat into silence, which is the quintessence of awareness."

Truth

The next day, I showed Temerlen my notes from our walk. I wanted to be sure I had caught his meaning.

After we had clarified a few points, he said, "Do you remember in the Gospels where Pontius Pilate demands of Jesus: 'What is truth'? He wants a definition. Something tangible he can apply to the law. Pilate represents the mind insisting on explanations to suit its needs. In this case, Jesus doesn't say anything. He stands quietly and gazes at Pilate. He symbolizes awareness looking at the mind, being aware while looking, conscious of the fact that no concept will ever satisfy the mind's demands."

The Tone of The Lord's Prayer

One morning I started our session by asking Temerlen about the musical aspect of The Lord's Prayer.

"There's something about the rhythm of it," I said, "whether you say it alone or with a congregation. It has a steady beat. Do you know what I mean?"

Temerlen thought for a moment and replied: "There is a familiar cadence with which it's usually repeated. It sounds a little like a song. It's even-keeled. It never gets out of hand, never runs away with itself.

"Partly" he continued, "this has to do with its neutral language. There's no mention of gender. No mention of race. No mention of I, me, or mine. And even though you can take personal ownership of the prayer as you say it, there is nothing personal in the prayer itself. Nothing is yours. It's about 'us'. The prayer is also quiet. It speaks about enormous things, but it never dramatizes or exaggerates. It's very humble and self-contained.

"At the same time, it gains momentum as it

goes along. It gathers internal fortitude and creates unity. And as it does, it becomes more quiet. This is why the prayer can't be said from rote memorization. It demands that you dwell on each word, honor its quietue, and yield to something beyond the prayer itself. In this respect, praying is not so much about going anywhere or getting there, but returning somewhere. Returning right here, right now, with conscious awareness.

"The Lord's Prayer," he added, "is a bridge that enables awareness to come home to itself. It's a bridge designed for awareness to 'cross over' to conscious awareness."

As Temerlen paused, I interjected: "Is that what the prayer is asking for?"

He thought for a moment, then looked up: "We don't often think about the gigantic nature of the universe and all that goes on inside it, much less about our place and purpose in this enormous scheme. But when you think seriously about it, you realize that being a human on earth who asks 'God' for things indicates a shortsighted view of the universe. How could you possibly know what to ask for when you know so little about the universe?

"As we've said before," he continued, "the mind is remarkable, but it doesn't come close to comprehending the truth about the universe: how we exist, why we exist, and why our minds can even postulate this. Meanwhile, we think it's a matter of just asking for things. Even silly things like a car or team victory, as though God was Santa Claus.

"It reminds me," he said, "that 'Amen', which is appended to the Matthew version of The Lord's Prayer, means 'let it be so'. The prayer starts be asking, but ends by saying, 'let things be'. That's because awareness doesn't try to do anything or change anything or fix anything. I'm not even sure that it can. All it wants is to be fully aware—which is the greatest change of all."

The Mind Can Only Think God

One afternoon, we were discussing how the mind works, but the topic wasn't coming into focus. It seemed like our minds wouldn't work at the very moment we started talking about the mind. So Temerlen turned instead to how we perceive and how this affects the mind.

"For example," he said, "we see a tree and think, 'there's a tree', or, 'that's an oak tree', assuming we know something about it. But if we stop and focus on the tree—really notice it and see it without ready-made thoughts about 'trees'—it becomes apparent that we don't know the tree at all. Our knowing stops at its appearance and is limited by a mental catalogue of the kind of tree it is, where it grows, whether we like it or not. The tree itself, its origin, its place in nature, its purposes for existing—all those things lie beyond the mind's ability to fathom at once. The same thing is true about everything in nature. We see it, but we don't perceive it with any depth of comprehension.

"And it's certainly true about people," he continued. "We see people, remember their names, interact with them, and think we know them. But there's more. Much, much more. And the planets, the sun, the galaxy? We know virtually nothing about them despite everything science claims. What then of an absolute God?

"All the mind can really do," said Temerlen, "is 'think' God. Its thinking is confined to a mental image that is learned, imitated, and assumed. The reality of God—whatever, wherever, however that is—lies far beyond the mind's reach. At best, the concept of God serves as a springboard to a higher level of awareness, the same way that prayer does. In both cases, the intent is not to stop at the literal meaning. The words are meant to propel the mind beyond itself, like a trampoline. A trampoline for awareness.

"A day or so ago," Temerlen continued, "we were talking about the song-like quality of The Lord's Prayer. It's like a religious chant that's meant to dizzy and numb the mind so the mind will give way to something else. But what if that was a method suited to earlier times than ours? What if The Lord's Prayer got introduced into western civilization for the same purpose, but with the intent to inform the mind rather than mesmerize it? What if it was meant to be used more consciously than a hypnotic chant?"

Temerlen grew silent and looked at me. I

looked back and shrugged to indicate that I didn't know. Inside I was stunned. Once again he had pulled the mental carpet from beneath me.

There was nothing I could say.

A Circle of Unity

Some mornings when we got together, Temerlen had a topic or point of view in mind. Sometimes he didn't. Or sometimes I would suggest something or introduce an idea to spark his thinking. One day, I made the comment: "It's interesting that the Lord's Prayer starts with the "Father" in his kingdom and ends with, 'for thine is the kingdom...'"

Temerlen set down his mug and said, "Yes, The Lord's Prayer is a circle. A circle of unity. It travels a long distance to end where it begins: in the 'kingdom'. It's as though it goes in search of itself, meets itself, gathers itself, and returns to itself. In fact, if you had to sum up the prayer, or if you had only two seconds and two words to say it with, they would be, 'Our Father'. Why? Because the whole thing is about awareness circumnavigating itself and returning to itself as conscious unity.

"It makes you wonder," he continued, "whether the mind is knowingly evoking conscious awareness, or if awareness is using the mind to evoke itself, to wake itself up to the reality that it is awareness. In the larger sense it doesn't matter which end you come at it from. The circle always starts and closes at the same point.

"The Lord's Prayer," he added, "is also not about the future. It's strictly about the present. On the surface, it seems to be about past and future. 'Come to us today. Forgive us for yesterday. Help us in the future'. But psychologically it's referring to being aware for the sake of being aware now. It purports no future. It's not about what may happen tomorrow, or about being a better person tomorrow, or about being saved tomorrow. It's about awareness consciously resurrecting itself *now.*"

Prayer as a Path

That day after lunch, Temerlen said he wanted to go back into the studio, which we did.

"The Lord's Prayer," he began, "is a path that leads to another dimension. Although praying takes place in the mind, it's meant to produce a result in a deeper place—a place of emptiness—where thoughts cannot go.

"This emptiness—this void inside—where awareness resides is 'the kingdom'. This kingdom is placeless, formless, fathomless. It has no past or future, and not even a present. It encompasses the present, but it's not in the present. It's the very substance of awareness."

I chimed in: "But isn't the mind in the present and essentially trying to be present when it prays?"

"Now we're getting to the heart of it," said Temerlen. "And isn't it astonishing that conversations like this don't take place in church? You'd think this is what people need to know instead of just repeating words and accepting their literal meaning.

"To answer your question," he went on, "both the mind and the body exist in the present and have a past and future. The body enters into time, moves through time, and passes out of time. It appears out of nowhere, takes shape, and disappears. The mind can project a future, recall a past, and think about what's happening in the present.

"Meanwhile," said Temerlen, "awareness is beyond the body and mind, and beyond the physical universe. Awareness sees the past, present, and future as they unfold for the body and mind, but it resides beyond them, outside of what we call time. It's not only in another dimension of time; it *is* another dimension in which everything else—time, space, past, present, and future—exists, in the same way that everything in the universe resides within a boundless emptiness that encompasses it.

"In this respect, awareness is formless and timeless," he continued. "But it's more than emptiness. It's aware of the emptiness. In our case, the only thing usually wrong with awareness, if we can say that, is that it's unaware of being aware. It's un-enlightened, un-realized, un-awake. This is the Achilles' heel that prayer is meant to address. It's what The Lord's Prayer was designed for."

I then added, "And the mind is able to figure all this out?"

"Yes," replied Temerlen. "But there's more to it than that. The mind can't arrive at this truth on its own. Awareness has to recognize its own nature. This cognition takes place inside the conduit of the mind where it leaves a slight trace; a reflection of itself. As this happens enough times—as the reflection becomes stronger—the mind and awareness both get smarter about what's going on. That's when prayer starts to become more purposeful, more meaningful, more conscious."

Hidden Truth

Temerlen often reminded me that he was not discovering or uncovering anything new. People throughout history have hinted at the symbolism of prayer. But I had never seen The Lord's Prayer dissected with this degree of insight. Temerlen kept making more incisions and peeling back more layers until we got to where the prayer, at its core, had nothing to do with people on planet earth appealing to God in heaven. It was a self-contained exercise of awareness devoted to becoming more conscious. On the one hand, this completely dissolved religion as we know it. On the other, it revealed a whole new concept of what God and religion mean.

One morning, as we were settling into the studio to discuss why people go to church to pray, I posed the question: "The more you talk about it, the more valid the inner meaning of The Lord's Prayer seems. So why would it not be more known about and practiced this way?"

Temerlen looked at me as if to say, "You know this means we're going to have to delay our planned topic to talk about this?"

I grinned. He shifted in his chair and paused.

Then he said: "Think about all the religious wars right up to our time. Throughout history, humanity has seethed with religious controversy, much of it due to nothing more than disagreement about the meaning of words. It's like a legal case where the law is so general that both sides can bend the interpretation to their advantage. The mind is very clever. It can always prove itself right and prove the other side wrong. This power to be definitive is its strength, yet this is also its undoing because there's always more than one layer of truth.

"The same is true about religion," continued Temerlen, "and about prayer. There is not just one truth, one practice, one layer. There are many. But the mind gets fixated on one layer at the exclusion of all others and gets angry when someone rejects or disagrees with the layer it's fixated on.

"Most people," he continued, "get fixated on the most visible layer and can't see deeper than that. When you drill down to the core of all religions, they come to the same thing, yet nowhere is there more disagreement than about religion. Why? Because everyone is fixated on their version of their layer."

"And religion," I said, "is supposed to be about unity and forgiveness. Instead, it creates the opposite."

Temerlen paused, turned away slightly, and looked up as though peering into a new thought.

"It's hard to comprehend," he said, "why religion has this opposite effect. The best explanation I've heard comes from George Gurdjieff. He was an Armenian-Greek who promulgated ideas about higher consciousness. Gurdjieff's teaching presented a cosmological scheme of man, earth, and the universe, showing how they're all connected—all one. Within this universal whole, humanity exists on the surface of the earth for the purpose of receiving and transmitting influences coming from the galaxy, the sun, the planets, and the moon. Each person is a tiny follicle or antenna that receives these influences, is shaped by them physically and psychologically, and then re-transmits them.

"At the same time, each follicle contains the possibility of realizing its situation, becoming conscious of itself within the universal whole, and consciously reuniting with the source of the whole.

Gurdjieff stressed, however, that the individual doesn't become conscious. What becomes conscious is awareness, and this potential of awareness that resides in each of us is what makes human existence on earth so miraculous."

Temerlen stopped for a moment, folded his hands, and looked pensively to one side. He stayed that way for several minutes in silence. Finally, he began again:

"You asked why more people don't see The Lord's Prayer the way we're seeing it; why this way of looking at it is not more known. Gurdjieff explained that this knowledge is not kept from anyone. It's just that most people aren't interested enough to look beneath the top layer. For anyone who *is* willing to look, it's an endless discovery. But to travel any serious distance, you have to eventually give up the notion of who you are as a person. And that is something most people don't want to do.

"The farther you go internally," said Temerlen, "the more you embrace pure awareness and the more it embraces you. At a certain point, it can't be explained in words because it takes you beyond words—as prayer is meant to do."

Why Church?

One day during lunch, Temerlen and I were trying to decide what to discuss next. I then asked him: "Why do you think people go to church to pray? Why not just pray at home?"

Right away it sparked Temerlen:

"Churches were originally built," he said, "according to a model that mirrored the nature of the mind and the nature of awareness. From a busy city, you step into a corridor that serves as a buffer between the world outside and the sanctuary within. You pause in the entry, wipe your boots, remove your coat, and shake off your worldly concerns. Then you step into the church proper where the atmosphere changes from busyness and cacophony to quiet and calm. The inside of a church resonates with emptiness and silence in an atmosphere that was originally designed to beckon awareness.

"Some churches," he continued, "have an inner church or chapel—a church within the church. Some even have an inner chamber reserved for priests. Only those who are 'eligible' can go inside.

"Human nature is the same. We're designed to develop an outer crust—a personality—to confront the world at large. But we also possess the means to step inside our mind, into an entry hall of self-collectedness, before passing through another door into the quiet of awareness. Just as people inside a church keep mostly to themselves, so we keep to our deepest sense of self in pure awareness. This is our 'closet' and this is where conscious prayer is meant to lead.

"The construction of a church is a blueprint of our inner world. Whether you know it or not, the act of going into a church resonates with a familiarity of calm. A church—especially one of traditional architecture—acts like a mirror that reflects a quality of awareness we can't quite put into words. Entering a quiet church almost always affects us to some degree and we walk out feeling differently. Usually feeling lighter and better. All because a structure *contained* us for a little while.

"If we were more sensitive," continued Temerlen, "we would notice that this is true everywhere. The places we go, the buildings we enter, the homes we live in—all of them exert an influence on us. The beach brings one kind of influence. A mountain top another. A wheat field another. We are also affected differently by an office, an art gallery, a hospital, and a coffee shop. We are, as Gurdjieff said, tiny receptacles—sensitive follicles—and the slightest change in our environment has an influence on us that shapes our thoughts and mood and behavior.

"A church," he said, "is designed to have a specific effect. It's meant to elicit awareness in us in a way that will render awareness self-aware."

Temerlen paused in his unique way, and then said:

"Churches were originally designed to show awareness how to be aware, and how to remain self-aware back in the 'world'—back in the maze of the mind and the lure of the body."

As I soaked in his thought, Temerlen waited. Sometimes he did this as though knowing what I was going to ask, but sensing he could not continue until I did ask. So I asked: "But why a church building? What makes it so different?"

"The short answer," he began right away, "is that a church is mostly empty. Everything about its structure reinforces its emptiness. The empty air inside a church is exactly the same as the air outside. The difference is that the structure of the building gives shape to the emptiness. This was the concept behind the Pantheon in Rome. Hadrian, who designed it, wanted the structure to enclose an invisible sphere and give shape to it. Ideally, this is what a church should do for us—remind us how to use the mind to give shape to awareness.

"As we said a moment ago," he continued, "you can be inspired by the view from a mountaintop, along the coast, or in a large spread of flatlands. All these provide the chance to contemplate space and experience a consciousness of awareness within that space.

"Outdoor places evoke awareness of the universe outside, whereas a church is meant to evoke the universe inside. When you take away the idea of 'church', all you are left with is a box of empty space that temporarily gives that space shape and makes it comprehensible. Our body and mind are also a box. The shape doesn't matter. What matters is to comprehend the emptiness within. Or, more accurately, to be aware of being aware of the emptiness."

Temerlen then added: "Awareness resides in all

forms of life, yet it does not recognize itself in most life forms. Humans are different in that they include the possibility—the birthright—to realize the significance of awareness. In our first interview I said that everyone is usually aware to some degree, but few people are aware of being aware. They never examine what awareness is, where it comes from, and how incredible it is. Even most things inside the universe are not aware of being inside it. Perhaps even all the empty space is not aware of being aware of what it is. Something else needs to recognize itself being aware of all the fullness within all the emptiness. And for that to begin, the emptiness has to be contained. The mind of man is at least one place in the universe where this can happen.

"That's why it's not a stretch to say that human beings are specially designed containers conceived for this purpose: to temporarily contain the essential material of the universe so it can comprehend itself and transform itself as conscious self-awareness. In other words, so that it can return to and be reabsorbed as its source, 'the Father'."

Do Water and Sunlight Pray?

I did not see Temerlen for several days after that. I was busy with work while he went on a short trip. The day he returned, however, he picked up right where he had left off the previous session:

"If a drop of water in the ocean could pray," he began, "it would not pray for itself—for 'me' and 'my' drop. It would more likely pray that it be remembered as belonging to the vast ocean. Nor would a drop pray *to* the ocean, because the ocean is nothing other than drops which together make the ocean. They *are* the ocean and there is no ocean apart from them. The drops, then, would pray for themselves to BE conscious of themselves as the ocean.

"Likewise, if a ray of sunshine could pray, it would not pray to the sun as something separate from itself 'out' in space. It would appeal to itself as originating in, and manifesting as, the sun itself. For a beam of light, praying would be a means of rendering itself conscious of the fact that there are no rays without the sun, and no sun without rays, and that on a vast scale they are one.

"This also points to a different meaning of 'Our Father'—not as a larger, separate, superior entity, but as the whole which all the parts together comprise."

Gender and Unity in The Lord's Prayer

One morning, Temerlen returned to the idea of the neutrality of The Lord's Prayer.

"Other than the word 'Father', he said, "there is no gender in The Lord's Prayer. The focus is not on man or woman. It's not even on being human. In the original Greek, the term Father is also referred to as 'which', not 'who' ("Our Father which is in heaven"). This implied that the father is not a heavenly man but a celestial state of being that is neither male nor female. Knowingly or unknowingly, English grammarians altered one word—changing 'which' to 'who'—and the prayer suddenly focused on the person (the body and mind) instead of on awareness.

"Think what that did to western civilization," he added.

A few minutes later, Temerlen continued: "There is also no 'I', 'me', 'he', or 'she' in The Lord's Prayer. There is simply 'we' and 'us'. The whole of us, together. Literally, this means all of we human beings, which gets reinforced when a congregation says the prayer together. But beneath the words is a symbolic reference to what we are as a whole in our being. The whole of you or the whole of me is not a person or thought. It's awareness. But we're not normally aware of this. It doesn't occur to most people that that *which* they are is not their physical body or collection of mental thoughts.

"This is what Gurdjieff meant," continued Temerlen, "when he said 'man is legion'. As he described it, our thoughts, feelings, impulses, and desires each call themselves 'I' without knowing they are just one of many 'I's —'I' am hungry, 'I' am full, 'I' love you, 'I' hate you. 'I' like that idea. 'I' disagree with those people. 'I' am happy, 'I' am sad. The list goes on as each 'I', displacing the next, manifests as the whole of us, oblivious to the multitude of other 'I's lurking in our psychological universe.

"The human psyche is like a county fair with a lot of rides, games, and concession stands. We think we are each of them, and we get lost in each of them as we move through the fair.

"Obviously," he said, "The Lord's Prayer is not meant for this conglomeration. Prayer has to start from some semblance of psychological unity. Otherwise it's just a repetition of words by a few 'I's in us, and nothing ever changes."

After a moment, Temerlen continued:

"Unfortunately, The Lord's Prayer is often just repetition performed in the blind hope that things will get better and that someone—God—will make it better. Meanwhile, the truth of awareness and the consciousness of awareness is lost."

Life and Awareness

The more Temerlen and I got together, the more we talked about prayer and awareness as though these were topics of ordinary interest and concern. When I mentioned this to Temerlen, he went into a lengthy explanation.

"The more awareness becomes aware of being aware," said Temerlen, "the more ordinary these talks seem because the more you see how everything else about existence stems from awareness and is wrapped in awareness. The only reason why all this isn't ordinary is because awareness isn't ordinarily aware of itself. And the more you realize that, the more strange it seems. Without conscious awareness at the core of your existence, life is merely one diversion and distraction and frustration after another."

I responded, "But the world is intimidating. Everything seems so important. People are so busy. It all appears to have a great deal of meaning and value."

Temerlen thought for a moment, then said, "It's like the surface of a stormy ocean. Big waves. A lot of movement, power, noise, and spray. It looks threatening. But when you dive below, you discover that the surface is a thin slice of the ocean. You see that what's happening on the surface is simply the result of one dimension rubbing against another. The physical world we live in is really the rubbing and result of other things. It is where multiple influences within the galaxy meet and interchange, and it has a purpose, but *by itself* it doesn't mean anything.

"All visible life," said Temerlen, "is a transmission and re-transmission and manifestation of energy stemming from universal awareness. It's all imbued with awareness and given shape by awareness which assumes infinitely different forms as it circulates through its own vast body which we perceive as the universe, the galaxy, and the solar system.

"Somehow," he continued, "the human body and mind form a sacred vessel in which awareness can recognize itself, realize itself, and nourish itself.

"At the same time, everything that awareness perceives in the universe is both a manifestation and reflection of itself. It is all awareness communing with itself in infinite ways. It's virtually impossible to find words to explain what this means and how miraculous it is."

Different Religions

Temerlen's description of awareness as the 'source substance' and manifestation of all life eventually led us back to the topic of religion and how it takes so many different forms. I said, "How can there be so many different religions if their source and purpose are the same?"

To which Temerlen replied:

"Once prayer is seen as an avenue to conscious awareness, the idea of different religions—especially opposing ones—dissolves. If there is opposition, it means that religion and prayer are both being approached the wrong way, in a limited way, and for a purpose other than true religion. It also becomes apparent that true religion isn't about outward behavior or conduct. It's about aspiring to self-awareness. The definitions may differ. The locations may vary. The circumstances may be unalike. But dig deep enough and you will find that religion, with prayer at its core, is always the same. It's a journey into your 'closet'—the quiet place within—where awareness transcends the mind and reaffirms itself as unalloyed awareness.

"Every religion, no matter its outward form,"

said Temerlen, "is honest to the degree that it respects a place of seclusion in each human and holds this place as sacred, hallowed ground—'hallowed be thy name'. True religion boils down to God as awareness talking to itself, recollecting itself, and being itself as pure, uninterrupted awareness that is aware of being aware behind everything it is aware of. Without this conscious awareness behind everything else, the universe amounts to nothing. It's impossible to imagine the universe without it, and yet we know so little about it."

"Maybe," I said, "that's why history has been fraught with so many religious wars."

Temerlen nodded: "This, too, is seen and comprehended by conscious awareness. But the full explanation of why religion gets distorted and ends up causing essentially the opposite of what it was intended for would require a whole new set of recordings."

He then looked at me with a smile and said, "Maybe that can be your next book."

"Maybe," I said.

The Bible and Technology

Temerlen often ventured beyond The Lord's Prayer itself. As he said, "The New Testament is peppered with inner meaning. Different stories represent different realms of our inner world. The characters symbolize psychological tendencies and metaphysical possibilities."

I commented: "You make it sound like a guide book or set of instructions."

"I know what you mean," said Temerlen," but think about it. It can't be a guide book because that would be too rigid. The authors understood that story form would be better. For one thing, stories are fluid and human rather than rigid and fact based. Stories let you plug in analogies here and there without having to symbolize each character, each word, each action. Besides, The New Testament can't be too factual because it's not meant to be a guide book for the mind. It's meant to be a source of inspiration for awareness.

"But look what happens," he continued. "The mind latches onto the literal meaning, goes digging for physical proof, struggles to resolve contradictions, insists on pinning down dates, and generally interprets everything in physical terms, as history."

"I have to admit," I said. "It's hard to shake the history. Books and movies have pressed it pretty firmly into our heads."

After a moment, Temerlen replied: "I wonder if the inner truth of The New Testament was more accessible before the advent of cinema. As you read, the mind produces mental images, but cinema is different. It throws fully formed images at you so fast that they kidnap and hypnotize awareness before you know what's happening. The images from movies also linger in the mind longer, and with more ferocity, than images formed while reading.

"It has to do with light," he added. "You need light to read, of course, but during the process of reading the mind acts as its own projector. The optic nerve enables one part of the mind to create images and then deliver them to other parts. But with cinema the images not only arrive fully formed, they shoot through the eye and into the brain with electronic force. It's an immediate strike and it penetrates very deep."

I added: "As you were just saying that, I had the

image of a brain being shot with a barrage of bullets, as though there's something violent about it."

"Yes," said Temerlen, "movies are remarkable, but they can be destructive, especially when there is a rapid burst of images in succession. They hold hostage the mind's ability to accommodate awareness. The images pour in so fast that there's no room for awareness. All the mind knows is a wave of images rushing through it and the force of those waves leave a strong impression in the walls of the mind where the images linger. It's similar to severe stress which numbs the mind and deprives awareness of the chance to gather itself, contain itself, and realize itself.

"Smartphones do the same thing," he continued. "They kidnap the mind's ability to accommodate awareness. They remove, at least temporarily, the possibility for awareness to be self aware—and you can see this on people's faces."

I agreed: "A sort of glazed look, you mean?"

"Yes," said Temerlen. "What you're seeing is the absence of awareness. The converse is also true: we can see the presence of awareness. But awareness is invisible, so we don't really see it. What we see is the result of its absence or presence. But this says something important about the age we live in. A lot of people on the planet are spending a lot of time looking at screens—phones, computers, movies—and making awareness more of a prisoner than ever before."

Again Temerlen paused, before adding:

"Ever since the discovery of electricity, this effect of industrial images has gotten stronger and stronger, more extreme, more urgent, more 'electronic'. People are even starting to talk faster than the mind can understand. It all seems like part and parcel of the advancement of technology, but it's pushing awareness and the potential for conscious awareness further and further aside."

Where is The Kingdom?

Most mornings before we recorded a session, Temerlen and I had coffee and talked about the session ahead or just things in general. I learned that these informal talks often included rich material, so I started recording them, too. On one such occasion, Temerlen was standing at the window looking at the morning sky, his back turned to me.

I said in his direction, "We've talked a lot about the kingdom of heaven, and you said once that it's placeless, but is that it? Can we pin it down any further?"

Temerlen remained at the window looking out. He took a sip from his mug, turned around, walked to the chair across from me, and sat down. After a pause, he began:

"One of the most fascinating things Jesus says in the Gospels is that the kingdom of heaven is 'within you and without you.' How can this be? What did he mean? Or, rather, what did the author—or authors—want to convey? If the kingdom is a place, how can it be in two places at once? If it's a spiritual realm, what does it mean that it's in two places?

"The Lord's Prayer," Temerlen said, "seems to offer a hint because it says, 'thy kingdom come, thy will be done, in earth as it is in heaven'. Notice, first, that the English translation changes the original Greek from 'in' earth to 'on' earth. The word 'on' suggests earth as a physical place, whereas the word 'in' suggests a spiritual realm. The phrase 'in earth as it is in heaven' also suggests that the kingdom is not in two places but that it can come into and manifest in both. Jesus's statement that the kingdom is 'within you and without you' then makes sense. He was saying that the kingdom can manifest in different realms within us. For example, as awareness in thought and as pure awareness independent of thought.

"Let's do this," he continued. "Let's edit the prayer so it reads:

Thy kingdom come in earth as it is in heaven, and thy will be done in earth as it is in heaven.

"Loosely interpreted, this would mean, 'May awareness manifest itself within the mind as it does within itself; may it do so consciously in both realms'. Or, it could have been written as a command, or even a spell, like this:

Awareness, manifest yourself in the mind as you do in yourself, and be aware of doing so in both.

In either case, 'kingdom' refers to the influence of awareness and 'will' refers to a conscious intent behind it."

"The Lord's Prayer," he said, "is one of the most compact pieces of literature ever written, so it makes sense that the authors would have condensed it to read, 'Thy kingdom come, thy will be done, in earth as it is in heaven'.

I then asked, "And what about 'earth' and "heaven'?"

"In this case," said Temerlen, "'earth' represents the mind and 'heaven' represents the realm of awareness, which is also itself."

He saw my frown, and added, "Think of it this way: the universe is all the emptiness out in space; the large container in which space and everything else exists. Encompassing all of it is an awareness aware of being aware of it. Does that ease your concern?" he asked with a smile.

All I could do was nod 'yes'.

Temerlen got up from his chair and carried his mug back to the window where he stood looking out for a short time. Then he turned around, leaned against the window ledge, and said: "There's more to it than that."

"To what?" I asked.

"To the statement that the kingdom of heaven is within you and without you."

I looked at him, waiting.

"The surface meaning," he continued, "is legitimate in its own right. In this respect, the kingdom of heaven is both a realm of the physical universe and a realm of our spiritual world. It's literally inside us and outside us. What's so fascinating about Jesus's words is that they mean all of this all at the same time."

After a pause, he continued: "We have to remember that each word of the prayer was carefully selected for a precise purpose. For instance, the line we have been talking about says, "Thy kingdom *come* as it *is* in heaven'. In other words, awareness already *is* in the higher realm of 'heaven' and the prayer is appealing to it to *come into* the lower realm of the mind and *be* the same there—that is, to be fully aware of being aware while it passes through the mind."

I replied, "The Lord's Prayer is remarkable literature."

"The highest form of literature," added Temerlen. "The highest because it's meant to transcend itself. If prayer doesn't take you beyond itself, it hasn't done its job."

Line by Line

After dinner one evening, Temerlen telephoned to say he wanted to spend the next day examining each line and word of The Lord's Prayer. "We've been talking about it." he said. "I want to go through it word by word as carefully as we can."

That's where he started the next morning:

"There are two versions of The Lord's Prayer in the King James edition of the Gospels," said Temerlen. "One in Matthew and one in Luke. Both appear abruptly and end quickly. The Matthew version is 50 words if you don't include the doxology—the closing verse which was added later, along with the word 'Amen'. The Luke version is 58 words. They start and end the same, but four lines are different in the middle."

We laid the two printed versions on the table and compared them, which revealed how they differed and how some words have changed with modern usage. For example, the word 'which' has been replaced with 'who', and 'in' has been replaced with 'on'—just as Temerlen had mentioned in one of our previous talks.

MATTHEW 6:9-13	LUKE 11:2-4
Our Father *which* art in heaven,	Our Father *which* art in heaven,
hallowed be thy name.	Hallowed be thy name.
Thy kingdom come,	Thy kingdom come
thy will be done,	Thy will be done,
in earth as it is *in* heaven.	as *in* heaven, so *in* earth.
Give us this day our daily bread.	Give *us* day by day our daily bread.
And forgive us our debts, as we forgive our debtors.	And forgive *us* our sins; for *we* also forgive every one that is indebted to *us*.
And lead us not into temptation,	And lead *us* not into temptation;
but deliver us from evil:	But deliver *us* from evil.
For thine is the kingdom, and the power, and the glory, for ever. Amen.	

"The doxology," said Temerlen, "is thought to have its origin in Chronicles from The Old Testament:

Yours, O Lord, is the greatness and the power and the glory and the victory and the majesty, for all that is in the heavens and in the earth is yours. Yours is the kingdom, O Lord, and you are exalted as head above all.

"This is a beautiful and moving passage, isn't it?," he asked. "Notice how it also says '*in* the heavens and *in* the earth'. And in this case 'the Lord' refers to absolute God. It makes sense, doesn't it, that it would be incorporated into The Lord's Prayer?"

Temerlen then copied the lines of the Matthew version on a separate piece of paper and wrote an interpretation under each line as I watched:

Our Father
The source of our universal conscious awareness

which art in heaven
which resides in a dimension higher than that of body and mind

hallowed be the name
let us honor as holy this conscious awareness which is beyond thought and words

Thy kingdom come
May the influence of this higher dimension of awareness reach into lower realms

thy will be done
may this influence consciously produce self-awareness

in earth as it is in heaven
within the mind in the same way that it nourishes itself in its own realm

Give us this day our daily bread
Grant us in each moment the "super substantial food" of awareness

And forgive us our debts,
Acknowledge awareness in us as our birthright of being human

as we forgive our debtors.
in the same way that we acknowledge awareness in others (do unto others…)

Lead us not into temptation,
May we remember not to be lured into the illusion of identity in mind and body

but deliver us from evil:
Awareness, recover yourself when you notice that you have lost yourself in fascination with the mind, body, and physical world

For thine is the kingdom, and the power, and the glory, for ever.
Conscious awareness is the only true existence, the only legitimate form of power, and the only real form of glory throughout all time, space, and experience

Amen.
Let it be so. Let the ultimate truth reign.

After he was done, Temerlen studied what he had written and then stood back: "It's not very inspiring, is it? My attempt to bring out the deeper meaning is genuine, but it's too intellectual, too scientific. The poetry is gone. The prayer has lost its transcendent magic.

"One thing this shows," he continued, "is how The Lord's Prayer is not for the mind. It's for emotional inspiration. The words are just a platform. They're meant to give lift to inspiration and ultimately to awareness the same way wings are designed to lift, not just the airplane, but the passengers inside the plane and carry them somewhere. But it's still a useful exercise because it shows that this prayer, like all real prayers, is not about people on earth and God in heaven, or about good and bad. It's about the mind and awareness."

Looking again at the words, he said: "Just think what is involved in this short prayer. Our existence hinges on awareness either realizing itself or being completely appropriated by the mind and body."

Another Perspective

After lunch Temerlen wanted to revisit the rendering of his interpretation.

"On its surface," he began, "The Lord's Prayer is written from the perspective of mankind appealing to God for salvation. But what if we turn this around and consider how the prayer might look from the perspective of awareness?"

He wrote out a long interpretation on a piece of sketching paper that he liked to use for these occasions:

I am the father—the source—of all.

I reside in a higher, sacred dimension which is incomprehensible to the mind.

My kingdom—the substance of my awareness—radiates through all forms to which I give life.

This radiating of my Self is a conscious act, intended for the same purpose in the human mind as it has in its original realm of pure awareness.

> *I endow the source of this awareness as a birthright, with the understanding that those human beings who recognize its source and potential will recognize and honor the same in other human beings.*
>
> *You must know that simple awareness unaware of itself is easily lured into forgetfulness once it enters the dimension of human thoughts, feelings, and sensations.*
>
> *This tendency of awareness to lose itself in lower dimensions is a universal misstep that only "you" as conscious awareness can extricate yourself from.*
>
> *It must be this way so that awareness, becoming conscious of itself, can realize itself as the infinite source from which it springs.*

I read along as Temerlen wrote. When he finished we both stood rereading it in silence.

I commented: "It sounds like a manifesto."

"The tone," said Temerlen, "is certainly different than our attempt this morning. And it's all due to changing the perspective. What's so compelling about this one is that it casts The

Lord's Prayer as a meditation; as a self-conversation of awareness. This is not just the mind trying to invoke awareness. It's awareness using the mind as a device to breath life into itself."

"The Brahman," I said.

"Yes," said Temerlen. "It's hard to put into words the significance this gives to mankind. Unlike perhaps all other forms of life in the universe, humanity on earth houses the potential of the conscious source of the universe. The universe is an ocean and knows it, while awareness in us is a drop of water without knowing it. But each drop has the possibility of realizing it."

Temerlen was silent for a few moments and then said: "There's a beautiful analogy by the Japanese master, Shunryu Suzuki, who said that all the water passing down a river is one body until it reaches the cliff and then spills over the edge as a waterfall. During the 'fall' each drop gets separated and experiences itself as separate, but is reunited with the whole when it reaches the bottom and then resumes its course as one river."

I added, "It sounds a lot like the 'fall' of man."

Temerlen turned and looked at me, almost startled.

"Yes it does," he said. "And that's where The Lord's Prayer comes in. It serves both the drop of water and the river. It's meant to bring simple awareness back to the unity of conscious awareness."

"It's also interesting," he added, "that the word religion comes from the Latin *relegere,* which means 'go through again'. This fits exactly with the idea that, during its time in the mind and body, awareness is journeying through the circuit of its own conscious self-rediscovery."

As often happened when he uttered such things, we both remained silent for a long time.

"It seems clear," said Temerlen, "why Jesus advised the disciples to enter into their 'closet' when praying: reunification is so sacred that it can only take place in supreme silence."

After another pause, he added: "It's the void consciously returning to the void."

The Prayer in Reverse

Two days later, Temerlen came to the studio still thinking about how The Lord's Prayer could be said in other ways. After just a sip of coffee, he started:

"We can also turn The Lord's Prayer upside down and consider it as the mind inciting awareness to climb up from the bottom of the ladder as opposed to 'God' coming down from the top. He folded over the page of his sketchbook and started writing:

> *You are all, always have been, and always will be.*
>
> *Consciously lift yourself out of this dimension of limited perception by becoming aware of being aware, rather than fooled into believing yourself to be all the things you are aware of.*
>
> *Recognize this capacity in all human beings, and in doing so recognize yourself as the source of this capacity.*
>
> *Nourish conscious self-awareness each moment, both in the mind and unto yourself, all*

the while comprehending that doing so is your true nature.

Just the fact that the mind can conceive of you as an idea is a miracle to be cherished,

Especially considering that you emanate from, and are the origin—the conscious source—of everything.

We stood side by side silently rereading what Temerlen had written.

"This upside-down perspective," he said, "is particularly powerful in dispensing with the notion of a 'person' asking 'God' in 'heaven' for help. It shows a mind possessing enough wherewithal to recognize that awareness is able to be self aware, to self-realize, and transcend the mind completely."

Then he added: "This also implies the mind looking directly at awareness, which is unbelievable when you think about it. Or awareness looking at itself through the mind, using the mind as a mirror.

"Yes," he went on. "I think that's more accurate. Because how can the mind actually see awareness? It can't, because if it could, then it would be awareness, which it's not. We're back to awareness trying to look at itself, see itself, somehow communicate with itself. But it can't. All it can do is be aware of being aware."

"You make it sound," I said, "as though awareness is always trying to be more conscious of itself."

Temerlen turned and looked at me as intently as he ever had.

"Isn't that incredible?" he said. "Especially when you consider that it's taking place through the vehicle—the conduit—of what we call a human being."

A silence fell over the room. It was as though we were taking a slow, deep plunge into a lake of serene presence.

Bread, Debts, and Sins

Examining The Lord's Prayer from different perspectives kept us busy. We went over what Temerlen had written many times and sometimes he made adjustments. Occasionally he explained more about what he had written, but no new perceptions came to him until one morning when he said he wanted to examine the lines that differed in the two versions. Specifically, the lines about daily bread, debts, and sins:

MATTHEW	LUKE
Give us this day our daily bread. And forgive us our debts, as we forgive our debtors.	Give *us* day by day our daily bread. And forgive *us* our sins; for *we* also forgive every one that is indebted to *us*.

"The questions we want to ask now," said Temerlen, "are what is bread and why is it 'daily' bread, what is meant by forgiving debts, what do 'sins' represent, and how are they different from debts? And how are all of these tied to awareness becoming more conscious?

"The lines beginning with 'Give us this day'...," he added, "alter the pace and poetry of the prayer. Suddenly we've left the realm of 'heaven' and entered into 'earth'—into the mind. You feel it become denser and more plodding. It takes on a sense of duty. Why?"

After a moment, he continued:

"Let's start with daily bread. One thing apparent right away is that this line and the two that follow sound like a command. Before this the prayer was acknowledging the father coming from above. Suddenly it turns to an insistence on needs and requirements 'in' earth. The need is for daily bread and the requirement is about handling debts and debtors. Literally, we take this to mean that God is responsible for providing for us, that he should do it every day, and we should not have to worry about it. Debts refer to our indebtedness to God as well as to debts we owe others and that they owe us.

"On the surface," said Temerlen, "it sounds like these are the two fundamental principles of life on earth: trust in God to provide for you, and be a good person by forgiving debts that are owed to you. But in reality this doesn't have much to do with salvation. After all, if there's one thing that humans—even religious humans—are reluctant to forgive, it's financial obligations. Entire legal and banking systems are even designed to prevent forgiveness and not only punish indebtedness but take full advantage of it for the sake of profit.

"And where," asked Temerlen, "are all the other rules of religious life from the ten commandments? In The Lord's Prayer, everything has been condensed to bread and debts."

At that point, I asked: "What about the Luke version which uses the word 'sins' instead of 'debts'? After all, sinning and forgiving sins are central to Christianity?"

"Yes," agreed Temerlen. "And in some translations, the word 'debts' got replaced with either 'sins' or 'trespasses', such as, 'forgive us our us our trespasses (sins) as we forgive those who trespass (sin) against us'. This in itself is interesting because it raises the question, what are trespasses? When you trespass, you step over a boundary into someone else's property. What's that got to do with religious life?"

"What about," I asked, "when one person physically violates another person, or when we criticize or condemn someone? Or when we tread into their beliefs and impose our own?"

Temerlen thought for a moment, then added, "The question is, what do all these things represent psychologically, and how are they important spiritually—especially in terms of awareness? Why do 'bread' and 'debts' and 'sins' and 'trespasses' matter when it comes to conscious awareness?

"But before we explore that," he continued, "'let's look at the next verse where the prayer shifts from requirements to a plea for help:"

And lead us not into temptation,
but deliver us from evil.

"The first thing that strikes you," Temerlen said, "is the word 'temptation'. What is temptation? Is it just temptations of the flesh: lust, greed, power? And what about 'evil', which is a strong word. Does evil mean just things like doing harm to others, stealing, murder?

"Equally interesting," he said, "are the words 'lead' and 'deliver'. Why would God, as the prayer implies, lead us into temptation, whatever temptation means? And if it's not a good thing, why would he lead us into it in the first place? If it's a bad thing, but necessary for us to go through, why would we ask God not to lead us into it?

"The same thing applies to the word 'deliver'," he continued. "If, after succumbing to temptation, we fall into evil, what does it mean that God should deliver us from it? Why doesn't it say 'save' us from evil. 'Deliver' was chosen for a reason. And isn't it curious that the words 'evil' and 'live' and 'deliver'—at least in English—all contain the same letters? So does the word 'liver', which is an organ that filters and cleanses materials before they enter the blood stream. However you look at it, the word 'deliver' is packed with meaning. It's also the last verb in the prayer, so it holds a place of importance. For one thing, it puts the ultimate responsibility back on God and brings the prayer back where it started."

With this, Temerlen paused, stood calmly with his hands folded behind has waist, and studied the words in silence.

"What I see," he continued, "is that The Lord's Prayer starts in heaven, passes to earth, and penetrates hell, all the while imploring God to be there when we need him. Can this be interpreted literally?" he said, turning and looking at me.

I looked at him quizzically and turned my gaze toward the writing to ponder what he was asking. Right away he answered his own question.

"Yes," he said, "it can. But it doesn't do justice to the prayer. That's just its top layer. There's more inside. And it's startling to think that humanity has not tried more rigorously over thousands of years to get inside. But it also explains why religion has been the source of so much tension and destruction. The more literally prayer gets interpreted, the more harm it does, as we see today.

"One way I have tried to examine the language of this prayer," continued Temerlen, "is to look at its rhythm and meter. For example, if we break it down using iambic pentameter as a model, we get this:"

Temerlen again wrote down the Matthew version, minus the doxology, underlining which syllables should get the down beat. Next to each verse he wrote which realm or dimension he thought it represented:

Our Father which art in heaven, hallowed be thy name.	**Father** — source: pure conscious awareness
Thy kingdom come, thy will be done, in earth as it is in heaven.	**Heaven** — spirit: realm of awareness
Give us this day our daily bread. And forgive us our debts as we forgive our debtors.	**Earth** — mind: thoughts and emotions
And lead us not into temptation, but deliver us from evil.	**Hell** — physical body: desires and actions

"The more I look at this prayer," said Temerlen, "the more I marvel at its brevity. Here, it's even more obvious because it's in four verses of two phrases each, with each verse reflecting a different realm of awareness.

"The way I learned to say this prayer" he said, "was with a certain cadence. But you can also recite it with iambic meter where the second syllable gets the down beat, the emphasis. Just as with Shakespeare's lines, The Lord's Prayer is hard to say with iambic correctness, especially if you have the 'church' version impressed in your mind. But look at the nuances that reveal themselves when we use the iambic. The effect is almost impossible to describe. It's best to say the prayer over and over silently by yourself and keep in mind that these words are not directed to a man with a white beard in the sky, but to pure awareness."

He paused for several minutes as we each said the prayer to ourselves in silence. Then he said:

"Repeating the prayer this way has a purifying effect. What gets purified is awareness," he said. "It enables awareness to realize itself and return to itself—to consciously inhale itself.

"This," he added, "is the ultimate purpose of any true prayer."

The Identity of Awareness

Temerlen often reminded me of Johann Sebastian Bach. Just when I thought he had exhausted an idea, he would launch into several more elaborate passages. This happened the next day when he returned to the meaning of 'temptation' and 'evil'.

He took out the large paper he had written on the day before and said, "The two words 'temptation' and 'evil' carry enormous weight in religion. They reinforce other ideas, such as fear, guilt, punishment, the need for forgiveness, a sense of righteousness, and so on. And the odd thing is that people enjoy this. Offer people the chance to strip all these notions out of religion and they won't accept it. 'No', they'll say, 'we need our guilt and punishment and righteousness. After all, we're human'."

I commented: "And we're talking about thousands of years of thinking this way. You can't expect to change it."

Temerlen stood pensively for several minutes. Finally, he said:

"We can't expect to change it. It would be too

big of a change. But, we're living in an era of massive technological and social change, almost upheaval, which is opening a window that people want to look through to a new horizon of understanding. We can't force anyone to look. All we're trying to do is help open the window. It feels right to be doing this. It feels like we should 'fore-give' to others as we have been 'fore-given' to."

After a moment, he continued "The thing I want to look at today," he said, "is how the ideas of heaven, earth, and hell relate to 'temptation' and 'evil'. The more I examine the prayer, the more I see that it starts in 'heaven', passes into 'earth, and then into 'hell'. But what do these mean? Clearly, they don't mean the sky of heaven, the earth we stand on, or the hell underground. They refer to spiritual, psychological, and physical realms. The Lord's Prayer is concerned about awareness preserving itself as it travels through all of them."

Here, Temerlen paused in his customary way before continuing:

"The farther awareness plunges into lower realms, the more likely it is to disperse itself, lose itself, even fossilize itself in what it becomes aware of. This prayer is a reminder of that and a remedy to it. It's a remedy because the nature of awareness is such that, wherever it finds itself, it has the capacity to be aware of being aware in that place. The Lord's Prayer is a tool for invoking this capacity.

"For whatever reason," he continued, "the human being is a special type of container in which awareness both loses itself and is able to find itself."

Heaven and Earth

"As far as the realms," Temerlen said, "heaven is obviously the highest. The prayer begins by acknowledging the source and essentially says, 'may this pure form of awareness retain its purity and consciousness of itself while 'in' earth the same way it does in heaven. 'Earth' refers to the mind. In other words, as awareness enters into the realm of human thought and emotion, 'may' it stay conscious of itself as awareness and not fall prey to believing it is the thoughts and emotions that it encounters.

"It is 'in earth'," he continued, "that bread and debts become important. Why? Because 'bread' refers—as the original Greek suggests—to 'super substantial food'. This is not special food for the body, but for the mind. It's the substance of awareness and the possibility of being aware of being aware. The idea of 'day' is also significant because a day can be different for a cell, an insect, a person, a sun, or a galaxy. In other words, in different dimensions. In this case, the 'day' of 'bread' refers to each moment; to the three seconds it takes for us to breathe. It could even be written as 'give us this day (this moment) our daily breath (the possibility of conscious awareness in each moment)'.

"Likewise, 'debts' don't mean what you owe, but what you are due. They mean conferring awareness and knowledge about awareness. The 'father', the conscious source of awareness, naturally confers—for-gives—the potential of being consciously aware. Each human being who receives this possibility as a birthright is responsible in a similar way for acknowledging and nurturing it with respect in other human beings.

"This is far removed," he added, "from the idea of paying debts and forgiving others for not paying theirs. Instead, it's about honoring the potential of awareness to recognize, realize, and manifest itself as full conscious awareness. All of this refers to 'earth'—to the mind—and to the passage of awareness through the mind; through the psychological 'world' of man.

"This is also connected to the idea of asking forgiveness: 'fore-give-ness'. It's not about asking for our 'badness' to be dismissed. It means readying oneself for the actualization of conscious awareness. And in this sense, the only real 'sin' is not to eat the 'daily bread' which is fore-given us.

"Something else to notice," Temerlen said, "is how the previous line is written. It says, 'Thy will *be done* in earth as *it is* in heaven'. In other words, conscious awareness 'in earth'—that is, as it passes through the mind—has to be an act of will. It has to *be done,* whereas in 'heaven' awareness simply *is itself.*

"As itself, pure awareness is effortless, motionless, dynamically at rest."

Temptation and Evil

"Bread and debts are one thing," Temerlen explained. "Temptation and evil are another. Even though The Lord's Prayer doesn't mention hell, the words temptation and evil imply it. But what they really imply is a further plunging of awareness beyond the psychological mind and into the physical body. This is the land of 'temptation' where desire, lust, greed, power, and possessiveness try to rule awareness. Once awareness gets caught up in these sensations and actions, it's very hard to extricate itself.

"'Evil'," Temerlen said, "refers to the deepest form of immersion and identification. Awareness, already identified with the psychological world of the mind, now identifies itself *completely* with the world of physical matter, the body. It has left the spiritual realm of 'heaven' (as pure awareness), passed through the psychological realm of 'earth' (in thoughts and feelings), and become lodged in the physical torments of 'hell' (the body and its sensations).

"One of the most extreme aspects of 'hell' is when awareness gets so completely immersed in negative thoughts and feelings that awareness itself *becomes fuel for* those negative thoughts and feelings and *provides ignition* for them to vent and burn—to be expressed—verbally and physically *through* the body. The more the *super-substantial material* of awareness combusts this way, the more violent and destructive negativity becomes.

"Awareness," he repeated, "begins its 'descent' from heaven, one step removed from pure awareness. It then journeys through the realm of thoughts and emotions which inevitably claim awareness for themselves, *as themselves.* This is bad enough, but it is still the realm of 'temptation'. Full-fledged 'evil' happens when awareness reaches the 'hell' of being entirely 'lost' and fully appropriated by the body in which it is effectively 'buried', at least for a time.

"This is the critical point where it needs to be resurrected and 'delivered' back to itself, back to its origin.

"What is both remarkable and important to understand," said Temerlen, "is that only awareness can deliver itself from the 'hell' of unbridled identification. Awareness can be alerted, inspired, and reminded, but only awareness itself can 'resurrect' itself and render itself conscious again—that is, aware of being aware apart from whatever it is aware of. Great art, literature, and music are full of meaning which try to convey this fact and try to arouse this truth within us."

Temerlen paused and seemed to drift along a stream of peaceful thoughts that came whenever he was thinking and talking this way. After a few moments, he continued:

"To fully understand," he said, "what 'temptation' and 'evil' mean, we have to keep coming back to the realization that conscious awareness means awareness which is aware of being aware—knowingly aware. Unknowing awareness means awareness that is aware only *of* things, without being aware of itself as awareness. We see a tree and are aware of it, but awareness is not normally self-aware at the same time. The same is true when we see our thoughts, feelings, and physical sensations. We're aware of them but not aware of being aware of them.

"Gurdjieff called this lack of conscious awareness 'identification' because it means that awareness has relinquished its awareness of being aware and given itself to—given its identity to—whatever it is aware *of,* be it something inside us or outside us.

"One moment awareness is identified with a thought that calls itself 'I'. The next minute it identifies with a feeling and calls that feeling 'I'. Then comes a physical sensation which it experiences as 'I'. The same thing happens when 'I' love a person or 'I' hate my job or 'I' am hungry or 'I' want that car.

"None of these is awareness itself, but because awareness is not aware of being aware *of them*, it establishes identity *in them* and makes them seem permanent when in fact they are only fleeting objects and mental images."

Temerlen continued: "The eastern mystics called identification 'attachment' to imply that awareness attaches itself to whatever it is aware of in the moment, with the result that it compromises—sacrifices—its ability to be aware of being aware.

"Restoring this ability is the focus of enlightenment, which means 'light within' or 'lit from within'. In other words, awareness aware of being aware."

Awareness is Elusive to Itself

"It's difficult to grasp," said Temerlen, "that even when awareness is conscious of being aware, it remains elusive to itself. That is, it does not see itself—just as the eye does not see itself seeing.

"Normally, awareness gets dispersed as consciousness *of* things. Even though it *can be* aware of being aware, it's the exception for awareness to knowingly, willingly, consciously sustain self-awareness. Doing so frequently or permanently is to be enlightened, self-realized, awake. There are different words for it, but they amount to the same thing—awareness aware of being aware behind everything else it is aware of.

"There's much more we can say about this," he added, "but for now it's enough to understand that this is what 'temptation' and 'evil' refer to. 'Temptation' means the naïve tendency of awareness to get lured into and appropriated by whatever it becomes aware of. We can even say that this is the greatest temptation in the universe.

"'Evil' then means the full capitulation of

awareness once it is absorbed by the thing it is aware of—a point of view, an ideology, a desire, a person, a fear. It doesn't matter what form it takes. What matters is that awareness lapses and loses consciousness of itself as awareness. All that remains is the thing it is aware of and a sense of identity in that thing. This is why Gurdjieff called it identification. Instead of being aware of being aware, awareness takes up residence—identity—in whatever it is aware of in the moment. And from this point of view, there is no greater evil in the universe. All other evils begin and end with this one."

Temerlen turned and looked at me with an indescribable expression. He was glowing with an intensity that gushed from some deep well of truth. He noticed my reaction—almost shock—and a smile crept over his face.

Then he continued:

"All of this shows how much meaning is contained in two words near the end of a terse prayer in the New Testament. Just two words. But they contain enormous knowledge. Once we understand what awareness is and the consequences of being aware of being aware—or *not* being aware of being aware—it becomes clear why awareness would not want to be led into 'temptation' and why it would want to be delivered from 'evil'. There's nothing more profound for the mind to pray for and nothing more sacred for awareness to strive for."

We became silent and Temerlen sensed that I was perplexed.

"Was it too much?" he asked. "Why that look?"

I hesitated at first, and then said: "It's just hard to see the mind as only a mechanism and not part of awareness or at least an expression of awareness. The body seems a little different. I get that it is separate. But I experience the mind as such a vital part of myself."

Temerlen put his hand under his chin and pondered for several long moments.

"You're right," he said. "It's puzzling. After all, we're using the mind to talk about this. The more we talk, the more the mind thinks it is awareness. But the mind can never know awareness. It can only know and talk about the concept of awareness. The same is true of God or some absolute awareness behind the universe. The mind can 'think' these things but never know or experience them directly."

After a pause, he continued:

"The body and its sensations are easier to see as something separate because they are more visible and palpable, whereas thoughts and emotions are less tangible. This is because the mind is closer to pure awareness, which makes it harder to distinguish from awareness and easier for awareness to be fooled by. You have to come to the realization that awareness can see the mind but not see itself; that it can only be aware of being aware; and that neither the body nor the mind have this capacity.

"But isn't it amazing that we can talk about this; that the mind can fashion a concept about it? And that doing so creates a channel for awareness to flow through? This is the real power of the mind, and even the mind can comprehend this to a certain extent. When it does, it has reached its greatest height. But that's it. That's the tiny tip at the top of the pyramid from where only awareness can launch into the pure void of itself.

"And, fortunately, it's something the mind can never fully grasp."

Slipping Out of the Mind

One morning, Temerlen surprised me with a simple analogy.

"The Lord's Prayer," he said, "is like a car. The mind gets in, turns on the engine, and starts driving. If everything goes according to plan and the driver knows what he's doing, there comes a point in the journey when awareness, which started the journey inside the mind, slips invisibly out of the mind—out of the driver's seat—and takes its rightful place in the passenger's seat as the simple witness of everything the mind drives by. The mind even knows when this happens, but it can't fully understand it because awareness is beyond the reach of words and concepts. There's simply a silent awareness of presence in the conscious void."

Temerlen seemed to be waiting for something. Then he added:

"At that point, the driver and car are no longer needed. But the question remains whether the passenger of awareness can stay in its conscious seat, or of it will get pulled back into the familiar comfort of the mind with which it has so long associated itself. If it can remain free, that is one thing. If it can't, then prayer still serves a purpose.

"Some people," he added, "keep relying on prayer because they like it. Slipping out of the mind and permanently occupying the passenger seat is not as easy at it sounds. And it may not even be completely possible until the death of the body, at which point there is simply nothing left for awareness to cling to or occupy.

"The crucial thing to understand," said Temerlen, "is that awareness is never seen or heard or felt. It doesn't think, speak, move, feel, or react. It is simply aware. And when it's conscious, it's aware of being aware.

"The problem is that the mind and body can't fathom this, so they keep trying to appropriate awareness. They also can't help it because awareness is what sustains them, even though they don't understand how. As awareness circulates through them, they assume they're aware, and that assumption becomes a feeling of 'I', 'me', 'mine'. The mind says, 'I am aware. I understand this. I am talking about it.' The body does the same: 'Look at me: I am being mindful. See me meditate. I am here and aware'.

"In all these cases however, awareness always remains just out of reach behind the scenes, neither thinking nor moving nor claiming a sense of 'I'. It has no tangible or visible form in either the physical or the psychological world. Awareness is conscious of the void of space that encompasses those worlds, and it perceives itself there, but it's not visible even to itself.

"This is highly significant," said Temerlen: "that awareness doesn't see itself; that it can be aware of being aware, but that it doesn't see itself the way it sees thoughts, feelings, sensations, people, and trees. At first this seems strange, doesn't it? But, as Jean Klein said, if awareness could see itself, it would not be what it is.

"This mysterious attribute has something to do with creation. Although awareness does not see itself, it sees everything else by means of the light of its own consciousness. This light reflects off everything it shines on and bounces back to awareness, which helps inform awareness about itself. In other words, by means of everything it perceives, awareness becomes aware of perceiving. That's its jumping-off point to become aware of being aware *as the perceiver.*

"Because awareness cannot see itself," he continued, "it has a naïve tendency—a natural 'temptation'—to associate itself with whatever it sees and is aware of. Thus the tendency toward 'temptation' and 'evil' which Gurdjieff called identification. And hence the need for awareness to realize that, although it can't see itself, it can be aware of itself—consciously self-aware, self-realized, enlightened, awakened, reunited with the source of itself."

Temerlen stopped for a moment. Maybe he noticed that I was overwhelmed by the avalanche of so much powerful information. Then he continued:

"Let's step back to something I said a moment ago: that all this has to do with creation. Try to envision an entire universe or even universes, and then imagine a source of absolute awareness encompassing them. If we consider that nothing in the universe can be perceived without this awareness, and that awareness realizes itself (becomes conscious of itself) by means of everything it sees getting reflected back to itself, this means that everything in creation stems from awareness, is tied to awareness, and nourishes awareness. Everything in creation serves the process of awareness becoming more and more conscious of being aware.

"Isn't that incredible?" he said.

Prodigal Awareness

I didn't see Temerlen the next day. He left me alone to transcribe the recordings and digest things for myself. When we did meet again, he returned to The Lord's Prayer with an added twist.

"The parable of the prodigal son," he said, "is an apt parallel to The Lord's Prayer. Think about it: a son comes to his father and asks to be given the inheritance he is due so he can establish himself on his own in the world. Isn't this the offspring of awareness—the son—saying to its source—the father—'for-give' (to) me what I am due—my birthright of awareness—so that I might venture into the world—into the mind and body—to prove myself capable of being aware of being aware on my own?"

I nodded. Then he continued:

"When you examine this story from the inside and inquire about its psychological meaning, a different realm opens up. In the case of the prodigal son, he leaves his father's 'kingdom' and enters the world—the mind and body— where he is immediately overcome by the lures of 'temptation' and 'evil'. In a short time he squanders his 'inheritance' and is ruined. Yet the story concludes with him being 'found again' and welcomed back in his father's 'house'—back where he started.

"For him to return, all it took," said Temerlen, "was acknowledgment by the son—by simple awareness—that he was lost; that in forgetting himself he had succumbed to the pull of all the things he became aware of in the world—in the mind and body. With this acknowledgment, he finds his way home again. In other words, by being aware of being aware, awareness dislodges itself from all it is lured by and finds itself back 'home'."

Temerlen paused as I let this impression of the prodigal son sink in. Finally, he said:

"There are two poignant images of The Prodigal Son by Rembrandt. One is a pen and wash drawing, the other is an etching. The first, which is less known, shows the prodigal son at the start of his journey. He's standing next to his father's desk watching his father sign over the inheritance he is due. The son is dressed in an elegant cape, with a sword at his side. He seems confident and excited. Through the window behind them, Rembrandt shows the son's horse packed for the journey. The skyline of the world awaits in the distance.

"The etching, on the other hand, is a popular depiction of the son returning home. He's hardly recognizable in a tattered robe. His hair is overgrown, dirty, and matted. His feet are bare as he kneels in the arms of his father who welcomes him with unconditional love. This story has been held up as an image of God forgiving and welcoming back into the flock one who gets tempted by the sins of the world—as long as they are willing to ask forgiveness. Less understood is that this parable refers to awareness returning to its source after having squandered its 'inheritance' as it journeyed through the 'world' of the mind and body."

"And what about the 'good' son?" I asked. "What does he represent?"

"Not only that," said Temerlen, "but why is there even a second son in the story? And why is he older? The story could have been about just one son, but it's about two—for a reason. Symbolically, the younger son represents immature awareness—awareness unaware of the value of its inheritance from the source. The younger son even says to his father, 'give me what falleth to me', meaning that which is due to me—my debt, my birthright. And, indeed, the father forgives him this debt, just as we see in The Lord's Prayer.

"The parable then says that the younger son 'wasted his substance'. Not his money or wealth, but his 'substance'. In other words, awareness is a rarefied substance that is wasted when it does not stay collected as itself, aware of being aware. This also fits with the idea of 'daily bread' in The Lord's Prayer. Bread is the same 'super substantial' material and it has to be used each day—each moment—or it will be wasted.

"Soon after squandering his substance," continued Temerlen, "the younger son 'comes to himself' and realizes he has 'sinned against heaven.' Heaven is the kingdom of heaven, the realm of awareness, and sinning means turning away from his substance. 'Coming to himself' means remembering himself, realizing his origin, and understanding how more than anything else he wants to return to the source—to full conscious awareness. At that point, the story says he 'arose and came to his father'. Awareness ascended to conscious awareness. And when he gets back, the father says, "This my son was dead and is alive again.' In other words, awareness completely forgot itself but has remembered itself and in doing so has 'delivered itself from evil' and is 'alive' again.

"Meanwhile," Temerlen added, "the older son is reminded by his father: 'thou art ever with me, and all that I have is thine.' The older son refers to mature awareness which has retained consciousness of itself as always part of the source. This is the lesson that mature awareness needs to learn—that *it is* the source. But this is a quieter lesson. There is no 'fatted calf' and 'celebration with friends'. It's a profoundly deeper recognition by pure awareness of its true nature and significance. It's like a drop of water in the ocean realizing that it is the ocean by comprehending that there is no ocean apart from all the drops in it."

After a pause, he said:

"The authors had a reason for including two sons in the story. They purposely made the prodigal son the immature one and the older son in need of a different kind of lesson which is much more subtle."

Temerlen took out the Bible and opened it to

the passage in Luke. He read it aloud in a slow whisper, occasionally pointing to and stressing the words he had emphasized in his explanation:

Luke 15:11–32

A certain man had two sons:

And the younger of them said to his father, Father, give me the portion of goods that falleth to me. And he divided unto them his living.

And not many days after the younger son gathered all together, and took his journey into a far country, and there wasted his substance with riotous living.

And when he had spent all, there arose a mighty famine in that land; and he began to be in want.

And he went and joined himself to a citizen of that country; and he sent him into his fields to feed swine.

And he would fain have filled his belly with the husks that the swine did eat: and no man gave unto him.

And when he came to himself, he said, How many hired servants of my father's have bread enough and to spare, and I perish with hunger!

I will arise and go to my father, and will say unto him, Father, I have sinned against heaven, and before thee,

And am no more worthy to be called thy son: make me as one of thy hired servants.

And he arose, and came to his father. But when he was yet a great way off, his father saw him, and had compassion, and ran, and fell on his neck, and kissed him.

And the son said unto him, Father, I have sinned against heaven, and in thy sight, and am no more worthy to be called thy son.

But the father said to his servants, Bring forth the best robe, and put it on him; and put a ring on his hand, and shoes on his feet:

And bring hither the fatted calf, and kill it; and let us eat, and be merry:

For this my son was dead, and is alive again;

he was lost, and is found. And they began to be merry.

Now his elder son was in the field: and as he came and drew nigh to the house, he heard music and dancing.

And he called one of the servants, and asked what these things meant.

And he said unto him, Thy brother is come; and thy father hath killed the fatted calf, because he hath received him safe and sound.

And he was angry, and would not go in: therefore came his father out, and entreated him.

And he answering said to his father, Lo, these many years do I serve thee, neither transgressed I at any time thy commandment: and yet thou never gavest me a kid, that I might make merry with my friends:

But as soon as this thy son was come, which hath devoured thy living with harlots, thou hast killed for him the fatted calf.

And he said unto him, Son, thou art ever

with me, and all that I have is thine.

It was meet that we should make merry, and be glad: for this thy brother was dead, and is alive again; and was lost, and is found.

As Temerlen read, goose bumps rippled across my body. When he finished, a hush fell over the room and we stood a long while in silence.

Sharing Insights

My usual practice was to listen to the recordings that Temerlen and I had made and transcribe them onto the computer. This way I had a full written and electronic record.

One morning, I was in the studio drinking coffee, reading back through the last few transcripts. Temerlen arrived, poured himself a cup of coffee, and took a seat across the room near the window where he liked to sit and look out. I eventually broke the silence:

"Do you ever wonder what people might think when they read all this? Don't you think the reaction might be pretty strong? I mean, you're more than upending the apple cart with your interpretations of The Lord's Prayer and the Prodigal Son and how everything ties to awareness."

Temerlen kept looking out the window, obviously pondering my question. Then he turned around to face me and said:

"I'm not really saying anything new. It's all been said before. Maybe what we're doing is bringing it together in a new way, a more complete way. And maybe that will have an impact."

He continued: "But I suppose for some people it might seem like we're eliminating the tax code or the entire tax system. Imagine, for example, how these ideas could affect all the churches—not just the religion side, but all the donations and tithing practices. What if people suddenly realized there is no one to confess to and no need to confess other than to their own awareness, which is, after all, what conscience is. What if they realized there's no man in the sky to forgive them or help them; that they rely solely on awareness, and that no one but them is responsible for awareness."

I replied: "Some people will call it blasphemy. Others will call you just crazy or arrogant."

"Or all three," said Temerlen.

After a long pause, he continued:

"But we have to consider—no, we have to give priority to—those who will take these insights to heart and see the implications. That might take a day or a year, or ten years, or 100 years, or longer. We don't know and we can't control that. What lies in our power is the understanding of how important it is to share these insights—to for-give them as they have been given to us."

Again he paused before continuing:

"It's like gymnastics or acrobatics," he said. "We jump onto someone's shoulders and then we help someone jump on ours. It's a delicate balance at each new height, but we have to keep making it go higher. We're talking about awareness becoming more and more consciously aware. Higher and higher. All the way back to its source, even though we can't comprehend all that that really means.

"There's nothing more worthwhile than this," he added. "No other pursuit or achievement on earth even comes close. This is what we have to remember. This is what fuels me to keep diving into pure awareness where there is nothing to hold onto."

As often happened, Temerlen's words dissolved my thoughts. I felt the urge to fill the void by saying something or asking him a question, and I was surprised to hear myself ask:

"Temerlen, what about you? Is awareness fully

developed in you? Is awareness self-realized the way you describe?"

Temerlen paused and lifted his head to look at me. His gaze was penetrating but gentle. He looked at me for several long seconds.

Finally, he said:

"You have to remember that it's always the mind that asks questions. And always the mind that answers them. Awareness never wonders, questions, or explains because it's endlessly silent, still, and void. It's just aware. That's all."

After a pause, he added:

"We talk about all this, we frame concepts around it, and we try to pin down the best words we can find. But that's all the work of the mind. Brilliant as it is, it's never awareness. The mind can never be aware. It doesn't recognize this about itself, but awareness does."

Then he added:

"It's also interesting how you put the question. You didn't say, 'are you self-realized'? You said, 'is awareness self-realized within you?' And that's the right way to ask the question because I, Temerlen, can never be self-realized. As Jean Klein said, awareness is not about the person; it's liberation from the person."

Awareness is Invisible

The next time we met, Temerlen returned briefly to the idea that awareness is invisible, silent, and motionless.

"The reason I want to talk more about this," he started, "is because we think awareness can be visible. For example, we think other people can see when we're aware or when awareness is present. But it's never true. At best, all we can see is the effect awareness has on the mind and body. It's important to remember this because even awareness has trouble realizing this about itself.

"The reason," he continued, "is because awareness has a quick, subtle effect on whatever it becomes aware of. It evokes an immediate degree of alertness or sensitivity which the mind and body experience as awareness. But attention, alertness, and sensitivity are not awareness. They're simply how the mind and body appropriate awareness.

"Think of it this way: as awareness passes through the mind and body, it vivifies them in the form of thoughts, feelings, and sensations. But those are results, not awareness itself. Nevertheless, they claim awareness and try to appropriate it. In the same way—and here's the thing I'm trying to emphasize—awareness appropriates them. As long as awareness is not aware of being aware, it knows only what it is aware of. This is the naiveté of awareness—that it's unaware, attached, identified, asleep. But this is very hard to catch because it happens in a flash each moment. As soon as a thought appears, awareness thinks it is thinking the thought, and the thought thinks it is aware. As soon as a pain appears, awareness thinks it feels the pain, and the pain thinks it is aware. This goes on every moment as awareness turns from one thing to another to another. And it continues every day until we die."

Temerlen paused, and then added:

"The whole picture changes when awareness becomes aware of being aware. Suddenly it realizes what it is. It starts to realize more and more clearly that it is not the thoughts, feelings, and sensations it perceives, and that they are not it. Conscious awareness just watches them unfold like a movie from the back of the theater.

"At first," said Temerlen, "awareness finds itself standing right in front of the screen, almost with its nose touching. That's better than being stuck to the screen or being sucked into the screen—which is what 'temptation' and 'evil' mean. But gradually, as awareness becomes more aware of being aware, it steps farther and farther away from the screen until it can see the entire screen from a distance, with an impartial gaze."

After a short pause, he continued: "You can't imagine how much room there is in our inner world. The universe inside is as vast as the universe outside. We just don't know about it and no one ever teaches us about it. But think what it means: we suppose we are living these lives when in reality awareness is watching these lives being lived. This changes the picture—and the whole meaning of life."

We sat in silence for several minutes. Temerlen looked out the window as I looked at him from the back. He seemed to be gazing outside, but I had the distinct impression that he was deep inside himself somewhere, maneuvering in all that space inside. Soon, he spoke again:

"I said that as awareness passes through the mind and body, it vivifies them. It gives them life, because without awareness we would be no more than an automaton. This is why robots will never get beyond a certain point because you can't program awareness into a robot. It's also why some people are so robotic: the ability of awareness to be aware of being aware in them has atrophied. They are vacant shells processing thoughts, performing actions, and appearing to be logical and methodical, but a critical effervescence is missing.

"Another remarkable thing about awareness is how it vivifies the natural world. Consider, for example, the flowers and trees before you become aware of them. Yes, they're there brimming with life, but something happens the moment awareness turns its focus on them. What happens is they 'reveal' themselves. The longer awareness remains aware of them, the more they reflect awareness back to itself, which reveals more about both them and about awareness.

"We can also look at it another way: the more awareness is consciously aware of something, the more it penetrates that thing. The next time you look at a flower or study a painting or listen to a piece of music, be aware of being aware as you do it and you'll notice that awareness permeates whatever it perceives. Or perhaps we can say that awareness expands itself to encompass what it perceives. It enlarges its field of awareness and absorbs what's in that field.

"This is true," he continued, "whether you're appreciating a flower, gazing at the ocean, looking at the sky, or peering into another person's eyes. Awareness embraces the thing it is aware of and includes the thing in itself."

After a pause, he added:

"Everything becomes awareness. Awareness includes everything. It is before, and after, and in everything. It's all one vast kingdom."

The Passenger

Two days later, Temerlen came to the studio after lunch. He was in 'clear spirits' as he liked to say. And he wanted to talk about Gurdjieff.

"The mind can't grasp that it cannot grasp awareness," he began. "It can think about awareness, it can produce a concept of it, but it can't know awareness and it certainly can't be awareness. As we have said before, something that becomes more and more obvious to awareness is that *nothing* is aware other than itself.

"Gurdjieff tried to explain it," he continued "with the example of a horse and carriage. He said that what we call our mind and body comprise not one brain but several brains, or as he called them, 'centers'. He used the analogy of a horse and carriage to explain what this means.

"The 'carriage' refers to the brain or center which governs our instinctive and moving self. The 'instinctive' center means the five senses and all the sensations they produce, while the 'moving' center refers to all our movements, most of which have to be learned. In Gurdjieff's analogy, the network of our instinctive and moving centers comprises the 'carriage'. The 'horse' then refers to the brain of our emotions which pull the carriage: 'I like, I dislike, I want, I'm afraid, I'm sad, I love you, I hate you, you're wrong, you should act differently'. All these emotions and the attitudes associated with them "push' and 'pull' the carriage of the body and sometimes run away with the carriage, causing great harm.

"Meanwhile, the 'driver' refers to our rational brain or intellect: the ability to think, reason, compare, choose, and decide. In this sense, a well trained driver has control of the reins and can steer the carriage wherever it wants to go.

"In right order, the driver controls the horse and the horse pulls the carriage. But think about it: the 'horse' of our emotions often rears up, runs off, and goes where it wants to go despite the intentions of our driver. And sometimes the 'driver' abandons its post or falls asleep at the wheel, in which case the horse does whatever it wants. Maybe it charges recklessly downhill at full speed. Maybe it stops altogether and just chews grass next to the road.

"Sometimes you even see people who are like a carriage all by itself. No driver (mind), no horse (emotions). Just a carriage (a body) sitting idle because there's nothing to pull or steer it.

"Why are we talking about this?" he asked rhetorically as he looked at me. "Because each of these centers—carriage, horse, and driver—think they are aware, that they are awareness.

"The carriage—our body—primps itself, takes pride in its appearance, criticizes itself, compares itself to other carriages, and so on. But without a horse and driver it's nothing and can go nowhere.

"Meanwhile, the horse—our emotional feeling of self—is strong and sensitive. It can pull a large load one minute, be highly empathetic the next, and easily spooked the next. The 'horse' in us is extremely sensitive but unpredictable. Even when it's been well trained, it can be easily provoked to jump the fence and run away—to exert a strong opinion or express intense anger. And, like the carriage, the horse's possibilities are limited without a driver to steer it, give it direction, and take care of it.

"Because the carriage and horse are so dependent on the 'driver', the driver is the most prone to assuming it is the conscious leader of the group. In other words, that it's awareness. But the driver fails to realize that it is dependent on a silent, invisible passenger—awareness—which hovers behind it and casts light on everything else: on the movements of the carriage and the behavior of the horse, as well as on the mind's thoughts, decisions, and formulations. Without the light of awareness, none of these could operate effectively.

"The opposite is also true: the more consciously awareness shines on the driver, the horse, and the carriage, the better they operate.

"In Gurdjieff's analogy, awareness is the 'passenger' in the empty seat, sitting quietly, looking out the window, watching events go by. This passenger is invisible to the driver, to the horse, and to the carriage, but they all feel the influence of its presence or lack of presence, and they act accordingly.

"When awareness is aware of being aware, the driver sits up straight, pays attention to where it's going, and skillfully steers the horse while knowing the limitations of the carriage. The horse may even have an emotional connection to its 'real' owner. But the carriage has the least sense of a separate passenger inside. In relation to awareness, the carriage—the body—is just a vehicle, a means to an end, even though it regards itself as conscious.

"As all this is going on in our lives, the carriage, horse, and driver also never understand that they exist separately from one another. They're usually intertwined. They overlap and operate together, sometimes for better, sometimes for worse. Meanwhile, our sense of 'I' and 'me' fluctuates between them, surging sometimes in one center, then in another, and again in another—in random, perpetual motion.

"The important thing to understand," said Temerlen, "is that whereas the passenger sees the driver, it is never seen by the driver, the horse, or the carriage. Awareness vivifies them and they feel this, but they're never aware of being aware. *The capacity to be self-aware is reserved for awareness alone.*

"But, as we've said before," he continued "the passenger also cannot see itself. It's simply aware of being in the carriage behind the horse and driver. It never *says anything* to the driver. It never tries to steer the horse. It doesn't directly guide the carriage. It just occupies its place as conscious awareness. But this has a tremendous effect. There's an enormous difference between an occupied and an unoccupied carriage."

Temerlen looked at me closely and said, "I know what you're thinking. You're thinking, what's this got to do with The Lord's Prayer?"

I smiled, of course, because I wasn't thinking that at all.

"What's so powerful about Gurdjieff's analogy," he said, "is that it demonstrates who prays and what prayer is for. It's tempting, isn't it, to think that the passenger would pray to 'God' in 'heaven'? But in our interpretation, it's the driver who prays. And what does the driver pray for? For the consciousness and welfare of the passenger.

"Here's another interesting thing," said Temerlen. "If you think about a conscious passenger, it works like this: the passenger of awareness influences the driver of the mind, which in turn guides the horse of emotions that pull the carriage of the body. But with prayer, the process is reversed: the carriage yields itself to the horse, which obeys the driver, who is appealing to and for the passenger. In other words, the body kneels, the emotions defer, and the mind gives ultimate control to awareness. 'Thy kingdom come. Thy will be done. Deliver us from evil. For thine is the kingdom and the power and the glory'."

Temerlen again paused and sat motionless for a time before continuing: "Have you ever wondered," he said, "where the passenger comes from, why it isn't always in its place in the back seat, and where it goes when it isn't there?"

I wanted to say, 'Of course, I wonder that all that time', but I didn't. Instead, I just looked at Temerlen, knowing that, fortunately, he would answer his own question.

"I don't know either," he said. "It's a great mystery. One idea is that the passenger is always there casting light on the driver, horse, and carriage—which makes sense because they could not function without it. Somehow, when awareness becomes aware of being aware—becomes aware of itself as awareness—the chemistry of the entire carriage-horse-driver changes. It's as though the whole apparatus gets plugged into a different circuit. And that's what prayer is designed to do. To plug us in.

"One way I see it," Temerlen continued, "is that

the passenger is normally lodged inside—identified with—the driver and therefore believing itself to be the mind. It also gets embedded in the horse and in the carriage. It infuses itself in all the centers and unwittingly takes itself to be all of them, but particularly the mind due to the mind's position in the whole arrangement.

"But when the driver appeals to the passenger to recognize itself, awareness can 'slip' out of the carriage, horse, and driver and assume its rightful place—its birthright—as pure conscious awareness.

"In terms of prayer," he added, "the carriage, horse, and driver embody the possibility for the passenger to become conscious of itself.

"We could also say that through existence in general, and through prayer specifically, awareness harnesses our body, mind, and emotions as a means for realizing itself.

"This," he added, "speaks to the profound nature of passing through the experience of being a human being."

Prayer, Meditation, and Yoga

The next morning, Temerlen arrived earlier than usual and started right where he had left off the day before:

"Everything we said yesterday about the carriage and horse, and about awareness and prayer, also applies to meditation.

"Ideally, meditation is prayer, designed to produce the same result. The person meditating is the driver whose goal is to create an inner atmosphere that is conducive to awareness. A mantra is simply a key, a reminder, for opening the door to one's inner 'closet' where awareness can coalesce and realize itself.

"When you understand this," Temerlen said, "you cease to think that 'I' am meditating, or that the goal is to shut down all thought, or that the end of meditation is an empty mind. You understand that meditation is a process of regulating all your functions—what Gurdjieff called 'centers'—for the sake of invoking awareness and inviting awareness to take its rightful place as conscious passenger.

"The same is true," he added, "about the pyramids. They're symbols of the same process. The four sides represent the four sides of human nature—the instinctive, moving, emotional, and intellectual 'centers'. The idea is to fold them 'up' into harmony so they meet at a point of unity. Their collaborative harmony is meant to spark pure awareness just above them. If you unfold a pyramid, it looks like a four-pointed star around a square base. That's man. That's our four brains or centers connected at the base, but operating independently. Fold them up together and something else becomes possible.

"Yoga," he continued, "refers to the same thing. Not the physical yoga that many people practice, but *pure* yoga which is intended as a physical and mental catalyst for inner stillness."

Temerlen paused for a moment, then stated with conviction: "The inner intent meaning of the different kinds of yoga was the same: to calm the body, still the mind, and purify the emotions, not for their own sake, but for the purpose of enabling awareness to empty itself into its own emptiness and retrieve itself from there again.

"In this sense, flexibility, stretching, breathing, and relaxing take on a very different meaning."

The Bible, Religion, and Light

After lunch, Temerlen returned to the carriage and driver analogy, but this time in the Bible.

"The Bible is a very sophisticated book," he began. "It seems to be a story or a series of stories, and some kind of record of facts. But it never sorts out completely. It never comes together as a clear whole. The Old Testament and New Testament are also fragmentary.

"But the more you study these books from the point of view of awareness," said Temerlen, "it becomes clear that the authors couldn't make them one contiguous story that plays out with perfect sequence and logic. That would feed right into the mind's tendency to confine everything to definitions, to eliminate contradictions, and to draw irrefutable conclusions—which is exactly what happens when you try to explain the Bible literally.

"Meanwhile," he continued, "the Bible, by design, is intended to be bits and fragments which logical mind can never piece together as a single whole, but which the discerning parts of our mind can intuit.

"As with The Lord's Prayer, the Bible was not crafted to convince our mind or to shape our morals. It was put down in a particular way for the express purpose of arousing awareness."

Temerlen grew quiet for several minutes. I again admired how he would fall into long stretches of reflection without the least sense of urgency to pin down a thought or express an idea. It was as though he was just watching his inner world drift by, or that he was finding his way along a tributary of thought until something became apparent and worthy of being expressed.

Finally, he said, "Isn't it interesting that Jesus is also called 'Christ' or 'the Christ' in the Gospels? Why two names? What does it mean? One way I see it is that Jesus represents the driver in Gurdjieff's analogy and that Christ represents the passenger of self-realized awareness. For instance, Jesus is tortured, crucified, and buried, while Christ resurrects and ascends to sit by his 'father'.

"The story," he added, "is a sketch, a blueprint, for prompting awareness to ascend to its source of conscious awareness. The more you study all the stories and 'miracles' in the Bible, the more you see they're about the success, failure, and maturation of awareness."

I then said, "Temerlen, I know you well enough to trust your perceptions when I hear this, but I think many people will think you're crazy now. You've already shredded the notion of God and prayer. Now you're taking Jesus away."

Temerlen lowered his gaze and then turned to look out the window. He sat quietly for a long time. I wanted to say something, but no words came. I felt an urge to get up and go pour a cup of coffee, but I couldn't move. I stayed in my chair looking out the window, too, then at Temerlen, and back out the window again. This went on for ten minutes as he pondered with palpable intensity.

"Religion," he finally said, "is a salve. Existence is difficult and it's even more difficult when awareness is rooted—stuck—in the body and mind. If religion can't unstick awareness, it can at least pacify the body and appease the mind. And it's good that it does.

"For many people," he continued, "religion is a display, a posturing, and a reassurance. It provides a sanctuary of psychological certainty and physical security. Meanwhile, people never jump out of the boat of their beliefs and dive into the depths. Nor do they feel any need to.

"Strangely," said Temerlen, "religion also becomes an impassioned reason to wield death and destruction. I say strange because this is the effect you would least expect from religion, yet it is perhaps the most common effect of religion throughout history. Also strange is that it's supposed to be this way.

"The design of the earth includes in its purpose an endless clash and destruction of human beings. And nothing is more potent than the ingredients of religion, which are extremely flammable. Depending on how it's handled, religion either implodes and takes everything down with it, or explodes and releases the essence of man, which is his awareness and its capacity to be aware of being aware.

"So in a sense," he continued, "you're right. When we tear away the surface of The Lord's Prayer, the Bible, and religion as a whole, we don't leave any remnants for the mind to use for itself. But you have to see this as lighting a fuse to help the whole thing explode so awareness can float free and return to its source.

"It's odd, isn't it," he said, "that religion destroys on the one hand, and that we're essentially destroying it—its literal meaning—on the other. I never thought about that before. Ultimately religion has to dissolve or be dissolved and both are necessary for the earth.

"Suffice it to say that we're caught up on the surface of the earth, which in turn is caught up in its orbit around the sun. Meanwhile the sun is locked in a circuit around the center of the galaxy and the galaxy is going who knows where for who knows what reason. Beyond that lies the void of one universe or perhaps infinite universes. What then of some absolute source of conscious awareness beyond everything else, and its blueprint for everything contained within it?

"Gurdjieff," Temerlen said, "referred to this ultimate source as the 'Absolute' and 'His Endlessness'. It's why The Lord's Prayer says 'hallowed be thy name' and 'Thine is the kingdom, and the power, and the glory, forever'.

"What makes life on earth so precious," he continued, "is that humanity provides an incubator where awareness can renew itself and return to self-realization as conscious awareness. This is what makes human beings one of the most sophisticated instruments in the known universe. A large part of this is due to the human eye and brain, and their combined ability to process the thing we call light, which is itself a mystery.

"Awareness and perception are very connected to light," said Temerlen, "and light can travel through many other mediums or forms such as gases, liquids, and even some solids. And yet, like awareness, light cannot be touched or held or even seen. Yes, we see the presumed source of light—lie the sun or a candle—but light itself is neither the source that it comes from nor the objects on which it falls or gets reflected.

"Light is an extraordinary, huge mystery. It may even be that suns are some kind of large generators and transformers, not just of light, but of awareness. Or perhaps light is a manifestation of awareness, or some aspect of awareness that the human mind cannot comprehend.

"All of this draws a very different picture of the universe, doesn't it?" he asked. "The universe becomes a single, enormous, interconnected body through which the mysterious substance of awareness gets transmitted, circulated, regulated, recharged, and transformed.

"It's unfathomable that we, in human form, can shape what we call thoughts about this and then filter those thoughts into what we call words. And that this capacity to use our organism for the self-realization of awareness is a birthright.

"What an incredible privilege it is that we can be a vehicle for awareness to consciously know and nurture itself."

World Without End

My talks with Temerlen covered many months which seemed like years. Even though I did most of the listening, it always felt like we were having a conversation. For me it was a lifetime of experience that enriched me beyond description. Consequently, it came as a blistering shock to learn one day that Temerlen was not well. Although his mind remained clear, his physical strength started to wane quickly and within a matter of weeks he grew very thin and weak.

I visited him in the hospital, but we rarely spoke. He mostly sat or lay in bed looking out the window, sometimes reading books he asked me to bring, or getting me to read to him. As you might imagine, foremost among these were the notes from our talks.

Even though Temerlen was seriously ill, he never looked despondent. On the contrary, he always lit up when I visited. Sometimes I sat next to his bed and held his hand or helped him drink, which became harder for him to do. At a certain point, as he had requested, we moved him to a hospice where he could be away from the "mess of medicine" as he called it.

Temerlen spent only three days at the hospice. Soon after arriving he lapsed into a deep state of rest that looked like a coma. All I could do was sit with him, hold his hand, stroke his head, and occasionally speak to him.

Late in the morning of the third day, the nurse said to me that it was almost time. It looked like Temerlen was about to go, she said.

I walked over to his bed and stood looking at the pale vestige of that previously shining face with its bright eyes now closed. The body lay motionless, its breathing barely discernible.

Suddenly, Temerlen took a deep, almost heaving breath. His eyes opened and looked at me with a depth of intensity and penetrating neutrality I had never seen before. It was as though he was peering at me with some extraordinary perspective from a great distance in the galaxy—as though he *was* the galaxy looking at me. His eyes stayed open and looking directly at me for several long minutes. Occasionally they shifted their gaze as though seeing something far in the distance. Then the light faded from them, and his head and body went limp. It was very clear that awareness had completely departed and left the vessel vacant.

After a minute or so, the nurse asked if I wanted to close Temerlen's eyes, which I did. It was a peculiar experience sliding his eyelids shut. We rarely touch another person's eye lids, where there is the sensation not only of the skin but of the eyeballs beneath, which are strangely palpable when there is no longer life behind them.

As I lifted my hand from Temerlen's face and stepped away from the bed, I expected to feel desperately sad. Instead, an indescribable void swept over me and engulfed my whole being, filling me up with serene affection and immeasurable gratitude.

I stood for a long moment feeling as though I had evaporated into air—"into thin air."

Temerlen and I had, of course, talked about death and about the implications of both life and death.

"Death," he once said," simply marks the end of a cycle during which awareness is exhaled and then inhaled by its source. Like the air in our lungs, it is 'breathed out' to be recycled, possibly for its own regeneration. During its journey, awareness remains free from everything it encounters in the mind and body, but it is nevertheless subject to being appropriated by them. That's where prayer comes in—as a sort of life vest tossed to awareness for its safety and well being during a disoriented journey through the world of mind and body."

I had also asked him, "What about the moment of death? What happens?"

"The actual moment of death," he replied, "appears to be and is swift because after its long exhalation, the draft of awareness, suddenly free of all burdens, is, within a fraction of a second, drawn back into the 'heart' of its origin. For all practical purposes, the identity which awareness embodied and traversed mentally and physically dissolves and disappears completely.

"In its place, pure awareness reveals and recognizes itself in the fullness of its own void as one world without end."

~ ~ ~

The real me remains yet untouched, untold,
    altogether unreached…

Walt Whitman